DAVID CRONENBERG

www.pocketessentials.com

First published in Great Britain 2000 by Pocket Essentials, 18 Coleswood Road, Harpenden, Herts, AL5 1EQ

Distributed in the USA by Trafalgar Square Publishing, P.O. Box 257, Howe Hill Road, North Pomfret, Vermont 05053

Copyright © John Costello 2000
Series Editor: Paul Duncan

A CIP catalogue record for this book is available from the British Library.

ISBN 1-903047-26-9

9 8 7 6 5 4 3 2 1

Book typeset by Pdunk
Printed and bound by Cox & Wyman

Something has happened to me: I can't doubt that any more. It came as an illness does... Once it was established, it didn't move any more, it lay low and I was able to persuade myself that there was nothing wrong with me, that it was a false alarm. And now it has started blossoming.
- Jean-Paul Sartre, La Nausée (Nausea)

The Outsider's case against society is very clear. All men and women have these dangerous, unnameable impulses, yet they keep up a pretence, to themselves, to others; their respectability, their philosophy, their religion, are all attempts to gloss over, to make look civilised and rational something that is savage, unorganised, irrational. He is an Outsider because he stands for Truth.
- Colin Wilson, The Outsider

for all true Outsiders

Acknowledgements:

My thanks to those without whom, etc.: Paul Duncan, Nigel Burrell, Marc Morris; and the rabid cinephiles: Mick, Simon, Martin, Dave, Steve, Ray, Neil, Reg, and all my *compadres* in movies: past, present and future.

Contents

1. The Inhuman Condition

Surreality Bite

1998. Friday August 7th. Midnight. The Laemmle Theater on Sunset Boulevard. I'm here to see Darren Aronofsky's cult movie, *Pi*. I take a seat. A tall guy's head blocks my view. I move along the row.

I'm blown away by the movie – a low budget, monochrome, surreal SF thriller, bursting with energy and invention. Afterwards, I approach the elevator to the parking garage, making favourable mental comparisons with the Davids Cronenberg and Lynch. The doors start to close. I hesitate. From inside a pair of arms thrusts through, forcing them open. "Room for one more," booms an oddly familiar voice. I step in and although I stand six feet, I find myself staring up at a very Tall Guy. I hear myself saying "Thanks…Jeff."

Christ! It is! Jeff Goldblum! The doors close. My mind races away: *Omigod! You are trapped in a telepod with Seth Brundle. Look! He's tapping instructions into the wall keypad.* I quickly scan for flies. There's only the striking blonde he's with. I fight an irrational urge to whisper to her "Be afraid. Be very afraid." *Maybe he'll do his ceiling walk.* I sneak a nervous glance, and receive a genial smile in return. My treacherous mind snaps back into reality. *Relax! You're in an elevator, that's all. With Jeff Goldblum, NOT Seth Brundle.* I smile back. The doors open. I'm alone. I step out through… billowing smoke, into a … warehouse? *This isn't right.* Where are the cars? And who are these other people in my head?

The above anecdote is mainly true. I think…

Canadian Gothic

A bespectacled middle-aged man, stripped to the waist, rips open a young woman's schoolgirl blouse and strangles her; slicing open her abdomen, he pours in acid before slitting his own throat…

A man scans a volunteer's mind but succumbs to the other's mental force until, racked with seismic tremors of agony, his head literally explodes…

A woman reveals large abdominal sacs containing the immaculately-conceived children of her own tormented rage…

A man inserts a pulsating videotape into another's abdominal slit; withdrawing his hand, he regards, horror-stricken, a ticking organic grenade which blows him through the wall…

A drug-addled gynaecologist administers a fix to his identical twin brother before opening him up with grotesque customised surgical instruments…

A… What's wrong? Oh come on, you think that's bad? There's the young woman who becomes an unwitting modern vampire when a side effect of plastic surgery leaves her drawing human blood through a phallic spike which extrudes from her armpit; or the 'children' who batter a young schoolteacher to death in front of her class; or the junkie writer who rubs bug powder into an ecstatic giant beetle's talking asshole, or… okay, I'll stop.

Not the Marquis De Sade's notebooks, or Hitler's diaries. The perpetrator of these and other atrocities is actually mild-mannered Canadian David Cronenberg. Dubbed the Baron Of Blood, King Of Venereal Horror ("It's a small field, but at least I'm king of it.") and far, far worse, he has made some of the most confrontational films of the last thirty years, pushing that particular cinematic envelope farther than any other major director. Forget the superficial tabloidisms - Cronenberg is a genuine artist who unflinchingly explores regions of his psyche where most people fear to tread, and in the process has produced a body of work unparalleled in modern cinema. He is now recognised as an intellectual, erudite and deeply serious film-maker whose aim and impact goes way beyond transgressive images and subversive set pieces (though he is damn good at them).

He approaches his art head-on, like other visionary artists. For example, Marcel Duchamp, whose *Fountain* (a ready-made urinal, signed 'R Mutt') provoked such outrage when submitted to (and refused by) the New York Society For Independent Artists in 1917, but is now regarded as a liberating cornerstone of conceptual art. Writers like Vladimir Nabokov and William Burroughs, much admired by Cronenberg, who dared tackle taboo subjects like under-age sex, homosexuality and drug abuse back when they were dangerous, before they became hip. Photographers like Diane Arbus and Robert Mapplethorpe, whose challenging images have been accepted as art despite frenzied opposition.

As much artist/philosopher as film-maker, Cronenberg's horror is grounded in the metaphysical, amoral sensibility of the Gothic novel, the macabre illusions of French *Grand Guignol* theatre, Freudian psychoanalysis and Descartes' philosophy of an absolute mind/body split. Although a cineaste, most of his cited influences are literary. Surrealism, postmodernism and existentialist philosophies strongly influence his ideas. His central characters are often pure 'outsiders' who, either through a derangement of the senses, or induced mental/physical alteration, suffer loss of identity, delusions and tragic death (Cronenberg has often referred to himself as an outsider). The protagonist of Henri Barbusse's existential novel *L'Enfer (Hell)* summarises this crisis: "An immense confusion bewilders me. It is as if I could not see things as they were. *I see too deep and too much.*"

Cronenberg shares SF author Philip K Dick's profound unease that at any moment one might become aware of the 'studio set' and discern the drab cardboard greyness, or malevolent Consciousness, lurking behind existence (a hot movie sub-genre; witness *The Matrix, Dark City, Pi* and *Cube*). He also plays devil's advocate against his own media. *Videodrome*'s Brian O'Blivion, convinced that "Public life on television was more real than private life in the flesh" now seems a true 'media prophet.' The proliferation of TV docusoaps has led to artificial environments where disparate individuals are thrust together to live as bugs under the microscope. *The Truman Show* and *EdTV* are meant to be satires, but have been overtaken by reality. Dick and Cronenberg's question is, which one?

Cronenberg's work is a godsend to besieged auteur-theorists who contend that any serious evaluation of a film-maker's merits should focus on recurring themes and concerns discernible through their *oeuvre.* With Cronenberg, this is magnified to the level of obsession, in an ongoing 'Cronenberg Project.' Even better, his mise en scène (systemic elements including decor, lighting, camera placing and movement, editing etc.) formally compliments his challenging concepts (he aligns himself more with *auteurs* like Fellini than journeyman directors-for-hire). Excepting *Fast Company,* his films are links in a chain of psychological and philosophical exploration. As a schizophrenic half-scientist, half-artist, he studies metaphysics via physics; his 'Project' is to dissect not only the body, but the mind (and their complex relationship), to lay bare the psyche and examine it through the Looking-Glass.

Commentators love to establish even the most tenuous connections between an artist's life and work. Surrealist René Magritte dismissed speculation linking his mother's death by drowning, her nightdress wrapped around her head, with similar images in his work, but denying such an appetising link cannot dent its potency. Cronenberg has distanced himself from comparisons between his father's death and the body-centred horror and mind/body dualism of his films, but acknowledges its influence on him as a person: "After he died I felt quite haunted... (he) started to die physically but not mentally. The body went,

9

but the mind didn't. It was a very non-specific disease. It started as colitis and became a very bizarre inability of his body to process calcium. His bones started to become brittle. He would turn over in bed and break ribs. It was quite horrible... You look at yourself in the mirror and you see that you're dying. Your mind says 'Wait a minute. Why is this happening?' Your mind and body are so separated. It's almost an incomprehensible horror." A powerful image, illustrating the probable root of Cronenberg's thematic consistency; his Hamlet-like obsession with his father's death.

Cronenberg's work is overdue an updated, comprehensive critical analysis. I hope this book serves as an entertaining and informative whistle-stop tour of his unique cinematic universe.

Cronenbiography: Beware The Ides Of March

David Cronenberg was born on 15 March 1943 in Toronto. His father Milton wrote a column for the *Toronto Telegram* and short stories for magazines, and once ran a bookshop. His mother Esther was a pianist, accompanying The National Ballet. Though ostensibly Jewish, his parents were non-religious. His relaxed liberal arts upbringing stimulated him to read widely, and to write from an early age. At sixteen he received an encouraging letter from the *Magazine Of Fantasy And Science Fiction* for a short story which came close to being published, about a disfigured dwarf handyman living a reclusive existence in a boiler room, who can project himself into his treasured possession, a painting of a lively Parisian café. This prefigures certain themes revisited time and again in his films: shifting realities, transformation, unique mental ability, disease and disfigurement.

Interested in arts and sciences but unsure which to pursue, Cronenberg opted for the latter and in 1963 enrolled at the University Of Toronto. However, he spent most of his time with arts students, and he took first prize in a university short story writing competition. The following year he enrolled in Honors English. The course was much more suitable, and his fellow students were "crazy, passionate, well-read, excited about all the things I was excited about."

After a year touring Europe, he returned to a life-changing event. A fellow student named David Secter had somehow shot a feature called *Winter Kept Us Warm* (a line from T S Eliot), using some of Cronenberg's friends as actors, including Iain Ewing and Jack Messinger (who would appear in *Stereo, Crimes Of The Future* and *Rabid*). This hit

Cronenberg like a lightning bolt: "...it was astounding for me to realise that human beings made movies."

Because there were no film courses at university he undertook his own research, through books and hanging out at the Canadian Motion Picture Equipment Company. In 1966 he shot his first surreal 16mm short *Transfer*, for Can.$300, handling the technical roles himself and using friends as actors. A year later he repeated the process with *From The Drain*, for Can.$500. From little acorns...

With Iain Ewing, Bob Fothergill and Ivan Reitman, Cronenberg started the Toronto Film Co-op. They spent many hours at Cinecity, a local arts cinema specialising in underground and European films, and the Cinethon – an all-night event where *Transfer* and *From The Drain* were screened.

While studying for his MA, Cronenberg remained infected by the film-making virus. Searching for ways to raise money, he applied for a writer's grant from the Canada Council because they had nothing similar for film. He was given Can.$3,500, which opened the way for his first major project.

Stereo stemmed from an outline about an experiment involving telepathy, which was then expanded during production. It eventually cost Can.$8,500, mainly because he shot on monochrome 35mm rather than 16mm, sacrificing location recording for image quality and dubbing the narration later. Again he was a one-man band – directing, writing, producing, photographing and editing, and using friends as actors. At 63 minutes, *Stereo* was ideal film festival material. Self-financed screenings at Edinburgh and Adelaide paid dividends when it was purchased for distribution by the owner of International Film Archives Of New York, who paid $10,000, and a further $5,000 advance against his next project. It attracted press attention and was screened at the New York Museum Of Modern Art.

A year later, with a further Can.$15,000 from The Canadian Film Development Corporation (CFDC), he shot *Crimes Of The Future* essentially the same way, upgrading to colour stock and complementing the narration with a strange soundtrack. It emerged as another science fiction avant-garde conundrum featuring the genuinely odd figure of Ronald Mlodzik. Cronenberg said, "Making films this way was kind of lonely. It was as close to cinematic poetry as you could get." Nevertheless, the virus had taken hold, and he gave up his studies.

He took another year out, living on a Canada Council grant in Tourettes-sur-Loup, a village in southern France. He attempted a novel,

11

but could not find his own voice above literary influences like Nabokov and Burroughs. He also shot a few 16mm television fillers for the Canadian Broadcasting Corporation. The shock of attending the Cannes Film Festival carrying his underground, 'art' films under his arm convinced Cronenberg that he would have to follow the commercial route. The problem was how to retain control when working with producers, larger budgets and other writers, and how to convince producers to take a chance on him in the first place.

Returning to Toronto, he continued to direct for the CBC; more fillers and a half-hour show for *Program X* called *Secret Weapons*, scripted by his friend Norman Snider, which aired in June 1972. Frustrated by the lack of a proper Canadian film industry, Cronenberg's search for a simpatico production company eventually led him to John Dunning and André Link's Cinepix. They made soft-core porn for the French-Canadian market, and responded to the odd sexual sensibility of *Stereo* and *Crimes Of The Future*. Cinepix originally considered Cronenberg for directing soft-core, but when he showed them a sex/horror script called *Orgy Of The Blood Parasites*, they saw its potential for the all-important American market. A three-year battle to overcome responses of disgust and revulsion and obtain funding from the CFDC ensued. This was a hugely frustrating period for Cronenberg, who was stricken by doubts it would ever happen and insecurity about his chances of directing, having discovered from Jonathan Demme that Cinepix had offered him the project in LA. Finally, the funding materialised and in August 1974 *Shivers* rolled in Montreal, with Dunning, Link and Ivan Reitman (after his low-budget 1973 exploitationer *Cannibal Girls*) producing on a budget of Can.$180,000.

The ram-raid impact of *Shivers* was powerful and immediate. After storming the 1975 Cannes Film Festival, it was sold to 35 countries and translated into 14 languages. Released in America as *They Came From Within*, English-speaking Canada as *The Parasite Murders*, and Quebec as *Frissons*, the shock wave caused by its uncompromising subject matter, full-on style and transgressive imagery was intense. Columnists and politicians heaped criticism on the CFDC for funding such filth; Robert Fulford's infamous *Saturday Night* piece, 'You Should Know How Bad This Film Is. After All, You Paid For It.' caused major waves. The first true Canadian horror film stuck a knife in the heart of its conservative, middle-class sensibilities. However, any publicity is good publicity, and the box office returns were spectacular - *Shivers* eventually grossed over $5 million!

Naturally, Cinepix clung on to its new star, and helped develop his embryonic script, *Mosquito*. In late 1975 he directed two half-hour shows for the CBC's *Peepshow* series, *The Victim* and *The Lie Chair*; the former pretty strong meat for television. Another crisis of confidence followed – about his script, and the negative impact of the controversy surrounding *Shivers* ("the whole episode probably cost me a year"). Dunning and Reitman convinced him to keep going, so after writing and directing a superior 30-minute film for the CBC, *The Italian Machine*, Cronenberg threw himself into the feature, retitled *Rabid*.

With much trepidation, the CFDC finally decided to finance *Rabid*, based primarily on *Shivers'* profits. Their collective nerves weren't eased when Reitman talked Cronenberg into casting porn star Marilyn Chambers in the lead role. In winter 1976 the cameras rolled for five weeks, again in Montreal; the budget Can.$530,000. Reitman's instincts proved correct – despite the post-*Shivers* backlash and lacklustre reviews, the film grossed more than $7 million, and was even distributed in America by Roger Corman's New World Pictures. David Cronenberg was suddenly Canadian cinema's hottest property.

At the same time, the government's tax-shelter initiative opened up the stagnant film market to private investors seeking tax breaks. The majority of personnel had to be Canadian, which meant box office problems as there were almost no bankable Canadian actors. Cronenberg's financial success ensured his popularity with potential investors. He was also itching to work, so when first-time producer Michael Lebowitz approached him to do a drag-racing movie called *Fast Company*, he agreed. The budget soared to Can.$1.2 million, and the film lensed in Calgary and Edmonton in 1978. It was Cronenberg's first feature using another writer's script, and he ended up doing last-minute rewrites. He and Lebowitz also had ideological clashes, something quite new to him.

Fast Company is widely regarded as the square peg in Cronenberg's rounded whole, having little in common with his more personal work. It sank without trace, as its US distributor folded before release and the rights became ensnared in litigation. On a positive note, Cronenberg formed connections with talented people who would remain loyal colleagues: Production Designer Carol Spier, Sound Recordist Bryan Day, Editor Ronald Sanders, and Mark Irwin, who photographed his next five movies.

Cronenberg began to develop a script about telepathy called *The Sensitives*, but a more personal script surfaced, reflecting many of the problems he was experiencing in his marriage and personal life. *The Brood* took over and five drafts later was drum-tight. Pierre David and Victor Solnicki's Mutual Films and the CFDC assembled a budget of Can.$1.4 million for a Toronto shoot. Released in 1979 to positive reviews, *The Brood* overcame unease about Cronenberg's previous films and the ever-controversial subject matter, to be regarded as a major artistic advance and a polished, mature work. Although less successful than *Shivers* and *Rabid*, *The Brood* impressed its producers and made a profit.

For his next project, Cronenberg revisited ideas dating back to *Stereo*, merging *The Sensitives* with an earlier concept, *Telepathy 2000*, to arrive at the outline for *Scanners*. Gentle progress was made until Solnicki and David (having formed Filmplan International with Claude Héroux) mined tax-shelter funding for a relatively immense Can.$4.1 million budget, provided that principal photography could be completed by the end of the tax year, December 1979.

Suddenly, Cronenberg faced the daunting prospect of shooting *Scanners* with almost no pre-production time and only a script outline: "I and my producers were really walking the tightrope together. There was a time when no one knew what was going on." The unrealistic principal photography deadline meant further weeks of 'second-unit' photography (i.e. cheating,) and an extensive post-production slog trying to obtain coherence in the editing room. But despite the severe pressure and more crises of confidence, the fast-paced science fiction thriller became an instant success upon its release in January 1981 - *Scanners* even topped the Variety chart in its first week.

Cronenberg's star rose steadily. Resurrecting an old treatment, *Network Of Blood*, he began his next script: "It had to do with a private television network subscribed to by strange, wealthy people who were willing to pay to see bizarre things." The early drafts of *Videodrome*, as it became, were pretty extreme and had to be considerably toned down in later versions. Pierre David somehow attracted investment and a distribution deal from Universal Pictures, and the budget escalated to Can.$6 million. The complex material proved elusive, even for Cronenberg, and not for the first time he struggled to stave off chaos. Many script alterations followed, through principal photography (October to Christmas Eve 1981) to post-production reshoots. Test screenings resulted in further restructuring and pick-up shots, and whole sequences were excised. Also, an X-rating meant cuts were required in order to meet Universal's demands of an R-rating.

Videodrome eventually opened in February 1983 and despite fairly solid notices and some rave reviews, died - pulled after its first two weeks, it grossed only $2 million. A mass audience could not engage with *Videodrome*'s radical departure from conventional narrative into confusing, hallucinatory realms. Andy Warhol perceptively called it "the *Clockwork Orange* of the 80s." Although *Videodrome* collected a Canadian Genie award for best film (shared, incredibly, with Bob Clark's *Porky's*), its provocative themes and images outraged conservative sensibilities, and once more Cronenberg was vilified by the moral majority as sick, twisted and dangerous. C'est la vie.

Desperate for a break from the intense dual pressures of scripting and directing when *Videodrome* wrapped, Cronenberg travelled to LA. In his friend John Landis' office he met Debra Hill, (producer of John Carpenter's *Halloween*) whose next outing was an adaptation of Stephen King's best-selling novel *The Dead Zone*. Coincidentally, he had discussed it in 1980 with Lorimar's Carol Baum when it was to be produced by Sydney Pollack. Although Cronenberg was interested, Lorimar opted for Stanley Donen and the project went into turnaround. Two years later it came full circle when Debra Hill offered him the job: "I immediately said, 'Yes.' I surprised myself."

Executive produced by Dino De Laurentiis, with a budget of $10 million, *The Dead Zone* was anticipated with curiosity: could this meeting of the 'Baron Of Blood' and the self-confessed "Big Mac of literature" work out? Cronenberg had rejected King's own script in favour of one by Jeffrey Boam; in summer 1982 he and Boam had brainstormed ideas, dispensing with King's slasher factor to concentrate on human drama and character. He acknowledged that his approach to the novel, coupled with the superior cast, constituted "a dipping of the toe into the mainstream."

The water seemed to his liking. Photography commenced in January 1983 near Toronto, at Niagara-On-The-Lake, and the film opened in October. Despite disappointing box office, *The Dead Zone* was an almost unqualified critical success.

Cronenberg was awarded a retrospective at the 1983 Toronto Film Festival, and invited to programme a Science Fiction Retrospective. Typically, his selections went way beyond accepted definitions of science fiction. The Academy Of Canadian Cinema published an excellent collection of critical essays, *The Shape Of Rage: The Films Of David Cronenberg*.

Revitalised and back in demand, Cronenberg had a choice of projects. Too much choice, as it transpired. Reluctantly abandoning his own insect comedy, *Six Legs*, as unworkable, and turning down many offers, he committed to *Alien* scribes Dan O'Bannon and Ronald Shusett's *Total Recall*, for De Laurentiis. One year later in Los Angeles, following visits to Rome and Tunisia and twelve script drafts, he quit the project in frustration (it was eventually filmed in 1990 by Paul Verhoeven for Carolco). After a brief cameo in Landis' *Into The Night*, he was thrown a lifeline when Mel Brooks asked him to remake the 1958 SF/horror film, *The Fly*. Having read Charles Edward Pogue's script and discovered parallels with his own ideas, Cronenberg agreed – on condition he had a free hand to rework it. Brooksfilms and 20th Century Fox posted a $10 million budget, and the production moved from LA to Toronto.

Cronenberg replaced first-time British director Robert Bierman. Brooks and producer Stuart Cornfeld looked to repeat their trick of attaching a director known for 'difficult,' singular material to a more accessible project, a tactic that had succeeded spectacularly with David Lynch's *The Elephant Man*. Brooks made it clear he wanted that David Cronenberg feeling; almost paraphrasing Hal Raglan in *The Brood*, he urged his director to "...go all the way. Let yourself go, and don't hold back." Cronenberg rewrote the script as an eccentric love story/tragedy, but insisted on a co-writer's credit for Pogue, whose script's potential secured his involvement. Having met Jeff Goldblum on *Into The Night*, Cronenberg cast him in the lead role, and convinced Cornfeld that Goldblum's lover Geena Davis should star opposite. The acting bug bit again - he made a cameo as a gynaecologist in the nightmare sequence.

The seamless blending of *The Dead Zone*'s feel for character with his earlier body-horror sensibility proved a potent combination. *The Fly* opened in August 1986 and became a critical and financial smash, its total revenue exceeding the sum of all his previous movies. Chris Walas and Stephan Dupuis received Oscars for special make-up and creature effects.

The Fly's box office practically guaranteed future financing and afforded Cronenberg access to the A-list slate. Being Cronenberg though, he turned his back on all that for a 'difficult' story which had haunted him for years: that of identical twin gynaecologists Stewart and Cyril Marcus, who died of drug overdoses five days apart in their plush but neglected New York apartment in 1975. Already the basis of Bari Wood and Jack Geasland's novel *Twins*, the Marcus brothers' story had been considered by Cronenberg and Carol Baum back in 1981. Old collaborator Norman Snider and *Klute* writer Andy Lewis had been commissioned to write drafts, but the project foundered. Five years later, Dino De Laurentiis' daughter Raffaella committed to Cronenberg's draft, as long as it could be kept under $10 million. While waiting for things to connect, Cronenberg engaged in a light TV workout, helming an episode of Paramount's *Friday The 13th* series.

Finding lead actors for *Twins* proved problematic – few wanted to risk the impact on their career of the sombre cocktail of sex, gynaecology and drug-taking. Jeremy Irons eventually agreed to take on the dual roles. When De Laurentiis Entertainment Group pulled out, near-bankrupt after the failure of movies like Lynch's *Dune* and *Blue Velvet*, Cronenberg found himself in a familiar crisis situation. Time ticked, costs mounted: the crew was kept on ice, property leases had to be paid to avoid demolishing expensive sets and Jeremy Irons was persuaded to wait. Cinematographer Mark Irwin was not, and jumped ship for a job in the States, much to Cronenberg's chagrin. Studios balked at the script and wanted it made lighter and less depressing ("Why gynaecologists? Why can't they be lawyers? Why do they have to die?") After almost a year of head-against-the-walls, Cronenberg and compatriot Marc Boyman struck a production deal with a consortium including Morgan Creek, Rank and Telefilm Canada. Boyman, part of *Twins*' initial impetus in 1981, now co-produced with Cronenberg on a budget of $9 million.

Rolling in February 1988, *Dead Ringers* was another interior piece foregrounding human strangeness and tragedy. (Old buddy Ivan Reitman appropriated the title *Twins* for his Hollywood Schwarzenegger vehicle. Already established, Reitman had become MegaHot after *Ghostbusters*.) Unlike *The Fly*, most of the traditional horror elements were downplayed, and *Dead Ringers*' mood of desolation and darkness was never likely to reach a large audience. Reviewers were not unappreciative, and the LA Film Critics voted Cronenberg Best Director, but as ever the content offended many: gynaecology became pornography, the Mantle twins' private hell glorified (i.e. dared to show) drug abuse and feminists cried misogyny, as they had against *Videodrome*. Yet again, Cronenberg's essentially realist approach to even the most bizarre scenarios was misinterpreted.

One project that had existed in the shadows for years was finally about to emerge into the light. Cronenberg had long coveted William Burroughs' form-breaking 1959 'novel,' *The Naked Lunch*, acknowledging its influence on his own work, but also its unfilmable nature. Anthony Balch and Stanley Kubrick were among many names associated with it down the years, but its seditious content and sabotage of narrative posed too many problems. In his introduction, Burroughs explained "The Sickness" of drug addiction: "I have no precise memory of writing (the book). The title was suggested by Jack Kerouac … The title means exactly what the words say: NAKED Lunch – a frozen moment when everyone sees what is on the end of every fork."

At the 1984 Toronto Film Festival, British producer Jeremy Thomas suggested to Cronenberg that they visit Tangier, where Burroughs wrote the book. In 1985 they made the trip, accompanied by Burroughs himself. Five years later, after directing two adaptations, Cronenberg felt the time was right. Also, Thomas' success with Bertolucci's *The Last Emperor* increased funding prospects.

While in England for his first substantial acting appearance, as a homicidal psychiatrist (who else?) in Clive Barker's *Nightbreed*, Cronenberg began the script. Realising the folly of attempting to translate the novel ("no culture could withstand that film"), he fused his own sensibility with that of Burroughs' life and work; in addition to *The Naked Lunch*, he included episodes from *Queer, Exterminator!* and *Letters To Allen Ginsberg*, plus the infamous real-life incident in 1951 when Burroughs killed his wife Joan in a drug-crazed attempt to shoot a glass off her head. By taking the text as an allegory about the process (and dangers) of writing itself, and the Tangier-inspired Interzone as a state of mind, Cronenberg found his angle on the material. At Christmas 1989 he sent the script to Burroughs, who was impressed.

Before going to England, he directed four 30-second commercials for Ontario Hydro. 1990 brought more commercials, for Cadbury Caramilk and an *Alien*-tinged Cronenberg Special for Nike trainers. He also directed two hour-long TV episodes of the CBC's *Scales Of Justice* series. A bonus arrived when he was invested as "Chevalier Of The Order Of Arts And Letters," by the French government, an honour bestowed on Burroughs years before.

Cronenberg's ex-DP Mark Irwin had told actor Peter Weller about *Naked Lunch* while shooting *Robocop 2*. Weller wrote to Cronenberg about his love of the book, and was subsequently offered the lead role. Thomas had to secure alternative finance when Japanese backers pulled out, and a mixture of Japanese, Canadian and UK money eventually comprised a $17 million budget. Filming commenced in January 1991. Then, the week before location photography was due to commence, war erupted in the Persian Gulf and insurance for Tangier evaporated. Carol Spier had almost no time to recreate Morocco in Toronto.

Upon its release in early 1992 it was hailed as a true Cronenburroughs hybrid; a successful commingling of film-maker's and author's blood.

Awards followed: eight Canadian Genies, including Best Picture, Best Director and Best Screenplay; the latter award also conferred by The Boston Society Of Film Critics, New York Critics Circle and National Society Of Film Critics. The NSFC added a Best Director gong. To coincide with the film's release, New York's Museum Of Modern Art held a Cronenberg retrospective. Critical success was never likely to be matched by box office, but an amoral victory was won. *Naked Lunch* the movie hit the world without being suppressed, or precipitating the apocalypse; transformed by North America's most controversial film-maker into a multi award-winning metafictional narrative. Funny old world.

Poised to adapt another landmark of literary notoriety, JG Ballard's searing 1973 novel *Crash*, which Thomas had optioned in 1975, Cronenberg opted instead for a relative time-out following the rigours of *Naked Lunch*. After parodying himself in an episode of the Canadian TV comedy *Maniac Mansion*, then playing a porn-obsessed carpet magnate in Don McKellar's short *Blue*, he refocussed on directing alone. When he heard about Warners' plans for David Geffen's hit Broadway production *M. Butterfly*, he read playwright David Henry Hwang's script. As it differed from the play, he thought Hwang might be open to experimenting, and registered his interest with Geffen.

Behind the play's Tony award-winning popularity, the subject (loosely based on real events) seemed ideal: a French diplomat falls for a Chinese diva in the Beijing Opera, but is he aware 'she' is really a he? Transformation: sexual, mental, cultural. A core Cronenberg theme. Geffen was glad to have Cronenberg, but wanted Hwang to script. As Cronenberg and Hwang were establishing a common wavelength, that was no problem. The budget was $17 million, and in late 1992 Cronenberg finally got to film abroad for the first time – in China, Hungary and France. Warners, Geffen and Hwang liked the finished film. The public, however, were distinctly underwhelmed. What had attracted theatregoers in droves failed to attract movie audiences. Like *Videodrome* and *Dead Ringers*, it fell between too many stools; not really a love story, not really a cultural epic, not at all a box office draw.

In 1992 Faber and Faber published *Cronenberg On Cronenberg*, a series of interviews by Chris Rodley. In March 1993, an all-inclusive retrospective of Cronenberg's film, TV and commercial work took place in Tokyo. Sponsored by Seibu department store, with the Canadian government, the province of Ontario and the Toronto Cinematheque, it included 'The Strange Objects Of David Cronenberg's Desire.' Among the 300 artefacts, posters, stills and props on exhibition were 16 Mugwumps and the Sex Blob from *Naked Lunch*.

More acting roles provided pleasant distractions: three films in 1994 (*Henry And Verlin, Boozecan* and *Trial By Jury*); two in 1995 (Gus Van Sant's *To Die For* and *Blood & Donuts*), and two more in 1996 (Landis' *The Stupids* and *Extreme Measures*) plus TV outings in *Moonshine Highway* and *The Newsroom*.

The real business remained his own films however, and after *M. Butterfly*, Cronenberg jumped straight back behind the wheel of *Crash*, again fusing himself and the author at the molecular level - after Cronenburroughs came Cronenballard. In transforming the novel he was careful not to dilute its impact; by retaining most of the shock elements, he guaranteed the film's notoriety. The finance was assembled from several independent sources by Robert Lantos' Alliance Communications and Jeremy Thomas. French company UGC withdrew after reading the script, and Fine Line only distributed in the US on the basis that they paid nothing until given the finished film.

Cronenberg transferred the setting from London to Toronto. The film's clinical, detached, unconcerned tone captures a spiritual ennui reminiscent of *Dead Ringers*, or *Videodrome*.

Crash won the Special Jury Prize at the 1996 Cannes Film Festival, for "audacity and innovation." It also won five Genies, including Best Director and Best Adapted Screenplay, and the Golden Reel for the biggest-grossing Canadian film of the year - major accolades for Cronenberg's "sex-and-wrecks" movie from a conservative, reactionary country that had once deplored his work. In the US however, entertainment mogul Ted Turner tried to stop his subsidiary company Fine Line releasing it because it disgusted him, and in Britain, an incredibly vituperative campaign was orchestrated against it by certain sections of the media and politicians. Cronenberg said at the time "...the English are so insane and their newspapers are so insane, and their politics are so crazed right now... They're completely obsessed with control... To say 'freedom' is like political suicide... the censor wants to pass the film uncut, but... he's afraid he'll lose his job; he's afraid that the government will take over censorship just as an excuse."

I saw *Crash* in Paris in 1996 on much the same assumption. (Amazingly, it was then screened at the London Film Festival, and Cronenberg and Ballard gave a Guardian lecture at the NFT.) The film was finally released in mid-1997, not with a bang but a whimper, and without causing anarchy in the UK. Form your own conclusions.

The acting continued: in *The Grace Of God* (1997), Don McKellar's excellent debut feature *Last Night* (1998), *Dead By Monday* and *Resurrection* (1999). In May 1998, New York's Thread Waxing Space Gallery held the "Spectacular Optical" exhibition, featuring artists who were influenced by, or shared affinities with, Cronenberg's work.

Cronenberg was developing two main post-*Crash* projects. When I spoke to him in 1996, he told me that his next project would revisit the theme and title of *Crimes Of The Future*, albeit substantially reworked. Also on his agenda was *eXistenZ*, his first original screenplay since *Videodrome*, inspired by the ongoing Muslim fatwa against Salman Rushdie for his 'blasphemous' novel, *The Satanic Verses*. Cronenberg interviewed Rushdie in 1995, and his imagination was galvanised by the idea of an artist forced by repressive groups or regimes to escape into hiding to stay alive.

By making his artist a computer game designer (but in a future/parallel world when computers and human biology have to a large extent been merged), and incorporating the game itself in the narrative, Cronenberg's examination of levels of reality and perception, and the dangers of creativity, continued ("...thematically, it connects to *Crash, Videodrome, Naked Lunch* and, in fact, *M. Butterfly*"). Robert Lantos' Alliance Atlantis organisation oversaw a budget of around $25 million. Interior photography took place in April and May 1998; exteriors around Toronto were shot in June. Released in early 1999, reviews were fairly positive and business was reasonable, but it felt lightweight, safe; certainly compared to *Crash*. Was Cronenberg becoming too comfortable?

Chairing the jury at the Cannes Film Festival in 1999, he was confronted by adopted Canadian Atom Egoyan for overlooking his film *Felicia's Journey*. When the fuming Egoyan threatened to punch him, with characteristic coolness Cronenberg responded, "That would certainly be one option."

The next instalment of the Cronenberg Project is eagerly anticipated. At the time of writing, *Red Cars* awaits the financial green light. Cronenberg loves fast cars and owns a Ferrari, so the life of the founder of the most famous marque in the world should be right up his circuit, so to speak.

This neatly encapsulates the paradox of David Cronenberg. Who is he really? Mild-mannered, bespectacled professor-next-door or Canadian Psycho? Racer or philosopher? Film-maker or public enemy? Whichever he is, he tackles his art head-on. Earlier films can be read as a vicarious wish-fulfilment of opposition to repressive social norms, in whatever guise it may come and regardless of how destructive its nature. His protagonists are merely helpless agents of chaos, transformed or destroyed by forces they cannot comprehend. The later, more 'mature' films interiorise this opposition; characters again defy conventional 'rules' of screenwriting, following their own personal white rabbits down holes leading inexorably to insanity or death, which is still preferable to mediocrity.

We should be grateful to David Cronenberg. He illustrates, in graphic detail, how precarious and untrustworthy the human condition really is. By showing the unshowable, speaking the unspeakable, he allows us to confront our demons, inhabit our nightmares and risk a peek into the abyss – *without actually going over the edge*.

2. Surrealism I: Emergence

Transfer (1966)

Director/Screenplay/Cinematographer/Editor David Cronenberg
Cast: Mort Ritts, Rafe Macpherson
Credits: Sound Margaret Hindson & Stephen Nosko; 7 minutes, 16mm, colour

Story: A psychiatrist is pursued by an obsessive former patient. They dine at a table placed (for no discernible reason) in a snowy field. The patient admits inventing details of his life in their sessions, but the psychiatrist failed to appreciate his efforts. The patient has come to value their relationship more than any other in his life.

From The Drain (1967)

Director/Screenplay/Cinematographer/Editor David Cronenberg
Cast: Mort Ritts, Stephen Nosko; 14 minutes, 16mm, colour

Story: The future. Two fully-clothed men sit in a bath at a home for war veterans. One breaks the ice; "Do you come here often?" He is a secret agent; the other an expert on chemical and biological warfare. They discuss changes to human and plant biology caused by the war. The agent takes notes as a mutated plant emerges from the drain and strangles the scientist. The dead man's shoes are thrown in a large closet with many others - there is evidently a conspiracy to murder survivors of the war in order to suppress information.

Comment: Cronenberg has described these early forays as "surrealist sketches for two people," likening the latter to a Samuel Beckett piece. He has also acknowledged his love of American underground film-makers like Jonas Mekas, Ed Emshwiller, Andy Warhol and Kenneth Anger, who may have influenced the visual dislocation and narrative ambiguity.

The characters' situation in *Transfer* prefigures the psychiatrist/patient relationship in *The Brood*, where Mike cannot bear the rejection when his "daddy" Dr Raglan commits totally to Nola's therapy.

Ultimately, Cronenberg remains philosophical about the standard of these building-block experiments, noting of *From The Drain*: "Like *Transfer* this is another early rambling of an adolescent film-maker. It's clumsy, awkward and technically not very good. I have tried to suppress the film and make certain that there are no prints available."

Well, he's done a damn good job. Although both films are catalogued in the University Of Toronto library their whereabouts are unknown, and enquiries are met with a metaphorical shrug of the shoulders.

3. Surrealism II: eXistenZialism

Stereo (1969)

Director/Screenplay/Producer/Cinematographer/Editor David Cronenberg
Cast: Ronald Mlodzik, Jack Messinger, Paul Mulholland, Iain Ewing, Arlene Mlodzik, Clara Meyer, Glenn McCauley
Credits: Production Company Emergent Films; Production Aides Stephen Nosko, Pedro McCormick, Janet Good; 63 minutes, 35mm b/w, 1.85:1

Story: A helicopter lands in a courtyard outside a large postmodern building. A man in a dark cloak disembarks. The soundtrack is blank except for voice-over narration which delivers comprehensive pseudo-scientific details of an experiment into various types of interactive experience ("human social cybernetics"). The title card indicates the film's exposure is 'restricted in accordance with the provisions of the Canadian Plastic Forms Act.'

The cloaked new arrival is one of eight "category A subjects who underwent pattern brain surgery" in a programme developed within the Canadian Academy For Erotic Enquiry's "organic computer dialectic system." This confers telepathic ability by a process of "biochemical induction;" the eight subjects have three months to prepare for their first group meeting. The architect of this experiment, eminent "aphrodisiast and theorist Dr Luther Stringfellow... exponent of the existential-organic approach to... socio-chemistry of the erotic," is strangely absent. Subjects walk or run down endless corridors, stroll through sunlit gardens, and interact without speaking. They form attachments to their researchers, a telepathic dependency which is also "an extreme form of psychic addiction." If they are removed from the object of their dependency for too long, severe psychic disorientation manifests itself. One subject drilled a hole in his forehead to "relieve himself of imagined cranial pressure."

A man undresses a woman and caresses an anatomical model while she sits blindfolded. Two others regard Tarot cards and contemplate symbols. The narrator speaks of a dominant telepathic personality that must learn to give way to the conglomerate. Others may try to avoid telepathic contact altogether by "schizophrenetic partition," conjuring a false telepathic self that induces images of morbid decay, vampirism and necrophilia in those nearby, and is notoriously difficult for the 'real' self to dislodge. Telepathic flow increases as the sensory bond between individuals grows. The conglomerate is expected to eventually displace the redundant nuclear family because of its adherence to principles of faith, love and dependency. On screen however, the only dependency appears to be narcotic.

Stringfellow's synthetic aphrodisiac drugs allow attainment of a full, three-dimensional sexuality, or "omnisexuality;" beyond restrictive concepts of hetero, homo, or bisexuality, a prototype of "three-dimensional man."

Over a slow motion semi-orgy, the narrator admits that the subjects - strangers who should have no telepathic flow – have denied their telepathic communication, when EEG monitors proved a very strong connection. Also, two of the eight committed suicide, and Stringfellow's absence may be explained by psychic dependency being reciprocal between telepathists and non-paranormals. Telepathic experience is characterised by pain and hallucination.

The narrator closes by stating that the data on the psychic interaction of the remaining six subjects has yet to be analysed.

Crimes Of The Future (1970)

Director/Screenplay/Producer/Cinematographer/Editor David Cronenberg
Cast: Ronald Mlodzik (Adrian Tripod), Jon Lidolt, Tania Zolty, Paul Mulholland, Jack Messinger, Iain Ewing, William Haslam, Ray Woodley, Rafe Macpherson, Willem Poolman, Donald Owen, Norman Snider, Stefan Czernecki
Credits: Production Company Emergent Films, With The Participation Of The Canadian Film Development Corporation; Production Assistant Stephen Nosko; Titles Jon Lidolt; 63 minutes, 35mm colour, 1.85:1
Story: The last surviving patient at The House Of Skin performs inexplicable rituals, observed by the Director, Adrian Tripod, and two interns. Strange, amphibian noises populate the soundtrack. Tripod's voice-over tells us the clinic treats "severely pathological skin conditions

induced by contemporary cosmetics," and was established by "the mad dermatologist, Antoine Rouge." Responsible for Rouge's Malady, a virulent disease which has decimated the post-pubertal female population, he has mysteriously disappeared. The odd, black-clad figure of Tripod wanders the futuristic corridors and courtyards of the clinic while the interns paint the patient's fingernails red. Although Tripod confesses he cannot discern their purposes, he is aware they have somehow taken over, and that "the House is undeniably in decline." He tastes a white foam which oozes from the patient; a symptom of the disease. Later, he licks blood from the dead patient's face.

At the Institute Of Neo-Venereal Disease, Tripod meets a patient, an ex-colleague who "was once a fierce sensualist, but has now become a pure metaphysician." An intern brings jars containing his preserved organs. He becomes melancholy when separated from these mysterious, non-functional growths; when they are surgically removed, he merely grows replacements. Tripod hazards his disease is "possibly a form of creative cancer."

Tripod is shown how to perform foot therapy by the Oceanic Podiatry Group, but he feels their evolutionary principles of tentacle, flipper, foot are "grossly distorting certain Rougeian concepts." While he practises his technique, a man clambers over a wall and attacks his subject. He watches helplessly as the man escapes back over the wall. He then attempts psychic therapy on a limping man's webbed-toed foot. The man shoves him away, and throws him a card.

On behalf of Metaphysical Import/Export, Tripod gives piles of clothing to men who arrange the items carefully into plastic bags. They appear to be candidates for executive positions, but Tripod has no idea of the significance of their incessant exercises. Upon visiting the man with webbed toes, whose limp is now cured, he is invited to join a group of heterosexual paedophiles; disciples of a new master, Tiomkin. Engaging psychically with Tiomkin's strange black spheres, or 'aquaria,' Tripod admits an attraction to "certain of these perverse, multi-dimensional images."

The Gynaecological Research Foundation asks Tripod to study a "research import," a six-year-old girl who has undergone prematurely induced puberty. The halls and corridors of the Foundation are patrolled by an unpredictable hired gunman, prone to mistaking certain social situations. Tripod takes his gun and chases the others.

At an obscure hotel for transients, also Rouge's last known whereabouts, Tripod secures accommodation for himself and his fellow subversives. His narration now refers to himself in the third person. The concierge shows them a "root-like excrescence" growing from his nostril. Tripod wonders if it could be a "modified antenna." Tripod is chosen to impregnate their captive before she can succumb to Rouge's Malady. He enters the girl's room, but senses the presence of... Antoine Rouge. He touches her face and licks the foam from his finger.

Comment: The first thing one can say with certainty about these early featurettes is that they are very strange indeed; the flip side of *Eraserhead*'s surreal, dream-like avant-garde coin. While Lynch gleefully climbs inside the nightmare, Cronenberg observes from a distance, sporting white lab coat, noting statistics on a clipboard. Lynch paints delirious surrealist audio/visual forms; Cronenberg examines the worlds of Kafka, Borges, Poe and Philip K Dick under a National Geographic microscope. This formal, detached approach echoes oblique European arthouse texts like Alain Resnais' *Last Year At Marienbad*, or Michelangelo Antonioni's *L'Avventura*, and its science-fictional use loosely connects with Jean-Luc Godard's *Alphaville*. Cronenberg admits "...a double billing of those two would take a lot of sitting through."

Although plainly the efforts of a young amateur attempting something Different, these hermetically-sealed dystopias are nonetheless remarkable. The spiritually bereft tone, cryptic narrative style and formal, abstract composition show an artist formulating ideas and setting parameters beyond restrictive boundaries of taste and moral decency. Although the films are quite introverted and personal, his intellectual rangefinder is always trained outwards: misanthropic, satirical bombs explode beneath social norms. If it is the artist's function to be an irritant to society, then Cronenberg succeeds from the get-go.

Stereo and *Crimes Of The Future* provide important insights into the unique Cronenbergian mindset, and introduce many obsessions given further flesh in later work. Telepathy/ESP is revisited in *Scanners*, *The Dead Zone*, *Naked Lunch* and *Secret Weapons*. The mind/body schism predominates, particularly in *Shivers*, *The Brood*, *Scanners*, *Videodrome*, *The Dead Zone* and *The Fly*; and is paralleled in the image/sound split of the featurettes. Sexual ambiguity, difference and deviation surface in *Shivers*, *Rabid*, *Videodrome*, *Naked Lunch*, *M. Butterfly* and *Crash*.

The Outsider might characterise almost all of Cronenberg's misfit protagonists. Chaos always lurks menacingly behind social order, ready to erupt. Scientific fallibility (especially when usurping 'natural' evolution), and/or the Absent Scientist motif are omnipresent (Cronenberg can be identified as *Stereo*'s Luther Stringfellow and *Crimes*' Antoine Rouge). Reincarnation, transformation, hacking away at countless taboos (including paedophilia in *Crimes Of The Future* and *Shivers*), disease, body horror, altered states, identity crises, alienation, man and machine, bizarre organisations, de(con)struction of the individual and/or the family unit - the list is an auteurist's dream (or nightmare).

Another notable element of the featurettes is their scathing humour. Revelling in a vicious parody of academic language, *Stereo*'s pseudo-scientific jargon overkill becomes acutely hilarious; the inflated, pompous narration is mocked by its discontinuity with the images on screen. Science is contaminated by occult emblems like the Tarot, and the controlled nature of the experiments is subtly ridiculed by the subjects' unpredictable behaviour. In *Crimes Of The Future*, these elements are taken to even greater extremes of absurdity. The wonderfully-named Adrian TriPOD (Mlodzik's effete intonation) wanders listlessly through an alien and alienating landscape, with neither destination nor ambition. He cannot comprehend the purposes of anyone, yet he aligns himself with each organisation, group or subversive faction he encounters. Existential angst for the chemistry set, as Cronenberg's identikit Kafka/Poe protagonist helplessly observes the decline of the House Of Skin (née Usher).

Sexuality is a key Cronenbergian theme; like his other themes, it is a reaction against Canadian "stifling order." Being British, and subject to a similar stiff-necked social blandness, the delicious irony of The Canadian Academy For Erotic Enquiry, or Institute Of Neo-Venereal Disease is not lost (recall Archie's impassioned speech to Wanda in *A Fish Called Wanda* about being English, "stifled by this dread of doing the wrong thing," and having "these piles of corpses to dinner." Now Cronenberg could really make something of that!)

His interrogation of sexuality was, and remains, a novel one. Why not a new sexuality for a new kind of human? Or an omnisexuality for "three-dimensional man"? Critic Robin Wood, perhaps failing to objectify his gay sensibility, regards *Stereo* as the only Cronenberg film to betray no sexual disgust, and positively connote homosexuality and bisexuality. Cronenberg simply uses telepathy as a point of departure from conventional forms of sexuality; "omnisexuality" is an inevitable consequence of telepathic ability. Anyone with direct access to the minds of others can discern and fulfil their innermost desires, whatever their orientation. Bodily sexuality may become secondary as new mental frontiers are engaged. In *Crimes Of The Future*, with the female population absent, the males must explore their own 'femaleness.' This is portrayed by mode of dress, gesture, use of make-up and the ever-ambivalent figure of Mlodzik, described by William Beard as "memorably fey and neurotic." ("I needed the correct fish for my aquarium," said Cronenberg.)

The mise en scène of these featurettes is the main difference from the commercial features. Long, languorous takes and angular architecture dominate. Saturated primary colours exist alongside claustrophobic blackness. A postmodern fragmentation is present throughout (and is carried into the features, one element that makes them so interesting); although the narratives do connect subliminally, they are puzzling and oblique, and Cronenberg deliberately withholds closure.

The title *Stereo* refers to extra-dimensional telepathic perception when compared to the monaural capacity of normal humans. *Crimes Of The Future* is slyly ambiguous: is it the future when the film's narrative is situated, after the scientific 'crime' responsible for the adult female population's demise; or the narrative's future when Tripod is (criminally) about to impregnate a six-year-old girl, who is moreover the reincarnation of his former mentor Antoine Rouge?

You want weird? You got it! Actually, you haven't – the films are not available. *Crimes* was released as an extra on the Criterion laserdisc edition of *Dead Ringers*, (but not on the DVD) and that's it. They serve as an invaluable and fascinating insight into Cronenberg's formative filmmaking phase, and should be seen. Are you reading this, distributors?

4. Body Horror: The Enemy Within

"Exterminate all rational thought" – Bill Lee (*Naked Lunch*)

Shivers (1975)

Director/Screenplay David Cronenberg
Cast: Paul Hampton (Dr Roger St Luc), Lynn Lowry (Forsythe), Joe Silver (Rollo Linsky), Allan Migicovsky (Nicholas Tudor), Susan Petrie (Janine Tudor), Barbara Steele (Betts), Ronald Mlodzik (Merrick), Fred Doederlein (Dr Emil Hobbes), Cathy Graham (Annabelle)
Credits: Production Company DAL Productions Ltd With The Participation Of The CFDC; Producers Ivan Reitman, John Dunning, André Link; Cinematographer Robert Saad; Editor Patrick Dodd; Music Ivan Reitman; Sound Michael Higgs; Special Make-Up And Creature Creation Joe Blasco; 87 minutes, 35mm colour, 1.85:1
Also Known As: They Came From Within, The Parasite Murders, Frissons

Story: At Starliner Towers, a modern apartment complex on Starliner Island, just outside Montreal, prospective tenants are welcomed by smarmy manager Merrick. In one of the apartments Dr Emil Hobbes attacks a young woman, Annabelle, who wears a school uniform. In another, Nicholas Tudor sits in front of a mirror, apparently suffering stomach convulsions. Hobbes strangles Annabelle, slices open her stomach and pours in acid before slitting his own throat.

Tudor goes to Annabelle's room and recoils from the scene of carnage. Later, resident doctor Roger St Luc is quite calm about it. Hobbes' partner Rollo Linsky describes their project, "a parasite that can take over the function of a human organ," and reveals Hobbes' penchant for paedophilia, telling St Luc he was caught "examining a girl's titties for breast cancer, in the faculty lounge, when she was 12 years old."

Nick Tudor's concerned wife Janine seeks advice from St Luc. Tudor leaves work early after more convulsions. He vomits what appears to be faeces over the balcony of his apartment, just as two old women pass below. It thumps onto one of the women's umbrella, startling them. "Poor birdie" remarks the other, examining the smear. The faecal parasite slithers away through the undergrowth.

In the laundry a woman investigates a trail of brown slime leading to a washing machine. As she lifts the lid, the parasite hurtles out and clamps onto her cheek. An elderly man complains to St Luc of stomach lumps, saying he may have caught them from "the girl in 1511" – Annabelle Brown. A distressed Janine Tudor visits her calming friend Betts. When she returns to the apartment, Nick has passed out. In a corridor two children play doorknocking pranks until a parasite appears in a letter box and they flee in terror.

Nick callously dismisses Janine's worry. He encourages his lumps to move, talking to them as one might talk to a pet. Betts runs a bath, listening to a radio announcement about the murder and suicide at Starliner Towers. In the surgery St Luc is indifferent to amorous advances from his nurse, Forsythe. They are interrupted by the telephone - Linsky has found Hobbes' personal notes, which far exceed their original project. Hobbes wrote: "Man is an animal that thinks too much," and his vision for the parasite was a "combination of aphrodisiac and venereal disease that will hopefully turn the world into one beautiful, mindless orgy." He was also using Annabelle as a guinea pig. St Luc admits he is aware of a few cases of stomach lumps already, and mentions Janine Tudor's husband. Linsky arranges to meet later in Tudor's apartment. Meanwhile Betts soaks in her bath, unaware of the parasite forcing its way up through the plughole and heading for the nearest orifice. The bathwater turns red as she thrashes in agony...

Chaos begins its inexorable ascendancy. Forsythe stabs a sex-crazed man who jumps her. A parasite attacks an old couple in a corridor before being impaled on the end of a walking frame. Assaults by residents on others are frequent. Nick attempts to seduce Janine, but she resists when she feels the lumps in his stomach. St Luc searches the garbage dumpsters in the basement for the parasite killed by the old man, but is ambushed. He overpowers his assailant, and unhesitatingly beats him to death.

Although afraid of what is happening to Nick, Janine is standing by her man... until a bloody parasite emerges from his mouth onto the pillow. In a state of shock, she runs to Betts. St Luc goes to Merrick's office and tells him to call the police. By now a zombie-like mob intent on sexual predacity is roaming Starliner Towers. In the basement car park, St Luc finds Forsythe about to be raped, and shoots the man in the back. Attempting to escape in a car, they are rammed by one of the 'crazies.'

A couple complains to Merrick about the disturbances. He ushers them into his office, where they are pounced on by a delirious group. Betts comforts Janine, stroking her hair and leaning close. As they kiss, the parasite exchange takes place.

St Luc and the injured Forsythe hide in the basement, waiting for the police. Linsky arrives at Tudor's apartment and finds the door open. Tudor is lying on the bed, his stomach seething with parasites. They fly at Linsky. As he tries to remove them he is attacked by Tudor, who tears a parasite from his face and crams it into his own mouth in an act of ownership.

In the basement Forsythe relates a dream about an old man: "...he tells me that even old flesh is erotic flesh, that disease is the love of two alien kinds of creatures for each other, that even dying is an act of eroticism." A parasite appears in her mouth. St Luc punches her unconscious. As he carries her along a corridor, the wall panels burst apart and a sea of arms breaks through, reaching for them. St Luc escapes and runs to Tudor's apartment. He encounters Tudor kneeling over Linsky's bloody corpse, and shoots him. He tries to escape but all the exits are locked. He makes his way to the indoor pool, and finds an open patio door. Sensing freedom, he runs up a grass bank but a line of the 'changed' slowly advances. Forced to retreat, he is pushed into the pool where Janine, Betts and Forsythe await. Many more join them, as he finally loses his struggle to remain 'human.'

5:26 a.m. A radio announcement describes a wave of unexplained sexual assaults across Montreal as a line of cars drive out of Starliner Towers, heading for the outside world...

Comment: The opening sales slideshow and deadpan voice-over directly recalls the cool form and style of *Stereo*, but then – bam! *Shivers* smacks you in the teeth with one of the most provocative sequences ever filmed. Hobbes' vicious, initially unexplained attack on a schoolgirl throws down a gauntlet. Cronenberg leaves the viewer in no doubt that, like the Terminator, he absolutely will... not... stop, and his sensibility-shredding horror career begins in earnest.

Themes: (Space dictates brevity, so lists are in no way exhaustive.) Cause And Effect: George Romero doesn't really explain how his zombies came to exist; nor does John Carpenter explain Michael Myers' superhuman abilities in *Halloween*. This is anathema to Cronenberg, who provides a rationale for even the most bizarre events. Frankenstein Syndrome/The Absent (Or Mad) Scientist: Scientific developments have unforeseen and unfortunate consequences. Hobbes unsuccessfully tries to destroy his own discovery before killing himself. Mind/Body Schism: The mind is the source of reason the body revolts against in Cronenbergian narratives. Bodily corruption leads to the downfall of reason and the rise of animal or primal behaviour. Even the improbably diffident St Luc kills with disturbing ease. The Mad Scientist invokes the Frankenstein theme; corruption by primal urges invokes Jekyll/Hyde. Altered States/ Transformation: Many horror texts centre on Gothic physical/mental change. All of Cronenberg's do. Postmodern/Existential Uncertainty: Is this the destruction or liberation of individual human identity? Cronenberg is not saying. Biological/Sexual Horror: Cronenberg has taken bodily repulsion farther than anyone. The parasites appear both phallic and excretory, and Betts' vaginal violation in the bathroom scene is calculated to provoke maximum disgust. Slaying Sacred Cows: Symbols of professional/social order (doctors, scientists, police) are fallible, mad, or helpless in the face of chaos. Secrets: Behind the bland façade of Starliner Towers lies the Pandoran secret of apocalyptic chaos. Bizarre Organisations: A fascination with odd corporate entities winds through Cronenberg's work. Starliner Towers is owned by the wonderfully monolithic-sounding General Structures Incorporated. Microcosm/Macrocosm: At the close, individual bodily corruption reaches outward to corrupt the body politic. Disease/Ageing/Death: Cronenberg's take - "There's a Latin quote that goes *'Timor mortis conturbat mea,'* which, roughly translated, means 'The fear of death disturbs me.' I think that death is the basis of all horror." Faithless: Cronenberg's characters are almost always irreligious. Locating horror in the body is therefore logical, with no spiritual battleground of 'good' versus 'evil,' and no promise of afterlife.

Style: Cronenberg's favourite shot is from below, framing characters in a slightly dislocated manner, or against claustrophobic ceilings. In *Shivers* this claustrophobia extends to the stifling apartment rooms. White predominates – clean, antiseptic. Red corrupts the cleanliness (the ultra-low shot of Tudor vomiting blood over the white toilet bowl is particularly effective). Black is used to startle, and black/white combinations to contrast. Stark horizontal and vertical lines bisect the frame, emphasising disintegration and tension. Cosy interiors and architectural lines connote human order which is gleefully ripped asunder as the 'plague' spreads.

Characters examine themselves in mirrors; knowingly after being changed, or presciently searching for some defect. Doorways frame action; as threshold, refuge, concealment of or portal to danger. The camera tracks down endless corridors, prowling toward the next assault, or flees in jerky hand-held panic. Modern art iconography adorns apartment walls (a Klee print of an abstract, misshapen human head is prominent). In St Luc's office, a wall sign reads "Sex is the invention of a clever venereal disease." Black humour lies behind Cronenberg's visceral horror.

The sea of arms bursting through the walls recalls Cocteau, and the line of crazies/zombies slowly advancing on St Luc is surely a nod to Romero. The final shot is a variation on the *Invasion Of The Body Snatchers* theme; this time, the 'changed' have the upper hand, and the infestation of human society is perhaps inevitable.

Cronenberg's mise en scène is always measured, precise, functional, formal. He eschews the pyrotechnics of visual stylists like Michael Mann, David Lynch, John Carpenter et al. He has never shot in cinemascope, and is not interested. He doesn't use storyboards, says he feels "physically sick" if a shot is not properly composed, and is renowned for knowing what he wants by the second take. In his quest "to show the unshowable, to speak the unspeakable," he has adopted almost documentary realist technique to portray the most disturbing, horrific, absurd, outrageous events; "I'm going to show you this is for real."

Trivia: Creature creator Joe Blasco turned down Romero's *Night Of The Living Dead*. *Shivers* was shot in Toronto's Nun's Island buildings, where Cronenberg lived ("We put up signs in the elevators asking people to donate their apartments"). The bathroom scene was shot in his living room! Cronenberg cast Lynn Lowry after noticing her in Romero's *The Crazies*. Scary European horror icon Barbara Steele threatened to punch him for slapping Sue Petrie (at her own request) to enable her to cry for a scene. The story stemmed from Cronenberg's dream about a spider emerging from a sleeping woman's mouth. The same year, *Crash* author JG Ballard wrote *High-Rise*, about the savage breakdown of social order within a tower block. Martin Scorsese saw *Shivers* at the 1975 Edinburgh Film Festival, and his famous Catholic sensibility was traumatised: "I made it through (the movie) in an ever increasing stupor of shock and depression. The last scene... is something I've never been able to shake. It's an ending that is genuinely shocking, subversive, surrealistic and probably something we all deserve."

Verdict: Horror movies by their very nature should be horrible, and *Shivers* certainly is. The combination of confrontational images, cinematic artistry, black humour and low-budget invention is a winning one. *Shivers* is an intelligent horror film that made me sit up and think "Wow, this guy is really going for the jugular!" Not for the *Scream*-ish. 3/5

"Go all the way through it, right to the end" - Dr Hal Raglan (*The Brood*)

Rabid (1976)

Director/Screenplay David Cronenberg
Cast: Marilyn Chambers (Rose), Frank Moore (Hart Read), Joe Silver (Murray Cypher), Howard Ryshpan (Dr Dan Keloid), Patricia Gage (Dr Roxanne Keloid), Susan Roman (Mindy Kent), J Roger Periard (Lloyd Walsh), Lynne Deragon (Nurse Louise), Victor Desy (Claude LePointe), John Gilbert (Dr Royce Gentry)
Credits: Production Company Cinema Entertainment Enterprises (For DAL Productions Ltd) With The Participation Of The CFDC; Producer John Dunning; Executive Producers André Link, Ivan Reitman; Cinematographer René Verzier; Editor Jean Lafleur; Music Ivan Reitman; Sound Richard Lightstone; Art Director Claude Marchand; Special Make-Up Design Joe Blasco Make-Up Associates; 91 minutes, 35mm colour, 1.85:1

Story: Hart and Rose speed along country roads on a motorcycle, dressed in black leathers. In the nearby Keloid Clinic, Murray Cypher pitches a promising franchising deal to Dr Dan Keloid and his wife/partner Roxanne. Keloid is unconvinced, afraid he'll become "the Colonel Sanders of plastic surgery."

A family in a camper van argues about directions. The husband turns the van just as Hart and Rose approach, fast. The bike careers into a field and Hart is thrown off. As it somersaults and lands on Rose the petrol tank explodes. At the clinic, a patient witnesses the accident through binoculars and runs for help. Rose is rushed to the clinic where Keloid performs emergency surgery. Roxanne is concerned – "Neutral field grafts have never been used internally. We could end up with a terminal cancer patient on our hands." He replies that he has no choice. In the operating theatre, he takes a sliver of skin from Rose's thigh. He explains that the grafting process will render the tissue "morphogenetically neutral," i.e. it will mimic the tissue of the area of the body where it is resited.

One Month Later. Rose lies in a coma. Before he leaves, Hart is told by Keloid that there is new tissue growth in her abdominal area.

Patient Lloyd Walsh examines his new face in a mirror. Rose sits upright and screams. When Lloyd investigates, she asks him to hold her. As she grips him tightly, something draws blood and he staggers for help. When examined, he can't remember what happened. The wound will not stop bleeding. Later, Rose awakes again and escapes into the night. In a cattle barn she lies next to a cow for warmth. A phallic red spike extrudes from her armpit and takes the cow's blood, but it proves unpalatable and she vomits. A drunken farmer enters the barn and advances towards her. She feeds before returning to the clinic.

Lloyd discharges himself from the clinic. Rose preys on a nurse in the jacuzzi. Lloyd hails a taxi and attacks the driver. The taxi leaps a bridge and is totalled by a truck on the freeway below. Rose telephones Hart and asks him to come as she's in trouble. He calls Murray Cypher to beg a ride. Keloid examines a strange vaginal/sphincteral orifice in Rose's armpit, and the spike strikes again. In a diner, the farmer from the barn attacks a waitress. While operating, Keloid takes a pair of scissors from a nurse; seizing her hand, he cuts off the top of her finger, clamping his mouth over the jetting blood as she screams.

Rose leaves the clinic. Murray and Hart drive past a line of police cars outside the diner as the radio news broadcasts the incident. They arrive to find the clinic crawling with police. Rose is given a ride by a truck driver. Murray is shocked as the berserk Keloid appears in the window of a police van, foaming at the mouth. Hart fears the worst when shown a woman's body in a freezer, but it is the nurse Rose killed.

Rose accepts a sandwich from the truck driver but is immediately nauseous. Later, a highway patrol officer checks the stationary truck; the driver is dazed and Rose is gone, having picked up another ride to Montreal. In a police station, Claude LePointe and his team of public health officials talk of an epidemic. The truck driver returns to the depot and attacks his colleagues.

34

Mindy Kent watches TV news of a "new strain" of rabies. The doorbell rings – Rose has come to visit her old friend. In the police station an officer foams at the mouth and growls. As Hart and Murray watch aghast, he attacks his colleagues and is shot dead.

Rose visits a sex cinema in downtown Montreal. A man moves to sit next to her. After sating her blood-hunger she leaves. In a limo, Claude LePointe warns a city official that the mayor "should be taking things more seriously." A truck blocks the road and two workmen appear; one plunges a pneumatic drill through the door into the chauffeur's leg. They drag him out of the car as the official takes the wheel and speeds away.

On TV, Dr Royce Gentry advocates martial law in Montreal: "Shooting down the victims is as good a way of handling them as we have got." Rose walks through a mall crowded with Christmas shoppers, followed by a man who sits next to her and makes small talk. He approaches another man for a light, and is attacked. The attacker is gunned down in front of Santa's grotto, as is the unfortunate Santa.

When Mindy arrives home, Rose is in blood-hunger. As Hart and Murray wait at a National Guard roadblock, dustcarts with men in white fallout suits hanging from them head for the city to assist with body disposal. Hart takes Murray home and goes to find Rose. When Murray goes inside, he is ambushed by his infected wife.

Mindy watches a TV broadcast about a 'carrier' of the disease; a person who transmits it but is immune, probably someone from the Keloid clinic. A maniac jumps on Hart's hood and is shot by marksmen. A fallout-suited figure disinfects the windscreen and waves Hart on. He arrives at the apartment and finds Rose feasting on Mindy. He tells her she is the carrier but she refuses to believe it. They struggle and he falls down the fire escape.

Rose picks up a man in the lobby and goes to his apartment. She dials Mindy's number. Hart hauls himself up the stairs to answer. She tells him she is conducting an experiment - if the man doesn't get sick then she is not the carrier. Hart knows what will happen and yells at her to get out, helplessly smashing the receiver as behind her the man sits up, foaming at the mouth.

Morning in the city. Sirens. Distant shots ring out. Rose's stiff, open-eyed body is thrown into a dustcart which slowly rolls away in search of more victims.

Comment: Rabid begins where *Shivers* ends. The horror again emanates from a single source, propelled by an episodic narrative, but this time chaos explodes onto city streets. William Beard notes "the epidemic as plot becomes the plot as epidemic." *Shivers* has no real protagonist, but *Rabid* has a sympathetic central figure. Rose is the unwitting Typhoid Mary who carries the plague without succumbing to it. She provides a human focus for the narrative, although her nihilistic fate leaves one with the Cronenberg trademark hollow feeling in the stomach.

Themes: Cause And Effect: As always, Cronenberg provides the origin of Rose's plight (except for deleting a scene where Keloid explains that the process he thought would replace her damaged organs has culminated in something completely different, thus leaving many people confused as to the nature of her new, bloodsucking organ). Frankenstein Syndrome/The Absent (Or Mad) Scientist: Man's hubristic complacency when dabbling in scientific hinterlands once again results in unforeseen (but to Cronenberg, dramaturgically inevitable) consequences. Keloid becomes a victim of his own interference in nature. Mind/Body Schism: As a result of this interference, Rose's body develops the curious blood-drawing organ, which her mind cannot comprehend but is nevertheless driven by. Cronenberg's interest in Emergent evolutionary principles is ubiquitous. Altered States/Transformation: Rose is first transformed by an accident, then by radical plastic surgery, before transforming others by infecting them. Postmodern/Existential Uncertainty: *Rabid* perfectly realises Yeats' classic lines 'Things fall apart; the centre cannot hold; mere anarchy is loosed upon the world.' Like Adrian Tripod, Rose's boyfriend Hart personifies certain existential characteristics; he spends much of the narrative trying to reach her, but when he finally does he is powerless to prevent her death. Resolution is only partially provided; we are shown Rose's fate, but denied the bigger picture. Following Frankenstein and Jekyll/Hyde motifs, Cronenberg gives the vampire myth a distinctly postmodern spin. In the apartment of the guy Rose picks up for her final 'experiment,' there is a split-head sculpture, echoing *Shivers* and foreshadowing *Scanners*. In the adult cinema, the soundtrack of the porn film features the line "Reality is like a dream." Body/Sexual Horror: Like *Crimes Of The Future*, a pus-like goo pours from victims' mouths. The outrageously dark humour of *Shivers*' gorefest is extended in memorable set pieces; Keloid cutting off the nurse's finger, the shopping mall Santa gunned down by the army, the construction workers' jackhammer attack on the chauffeur, the farmer tucking into a waitress as well as fried chicken. Rose's thorn is part phallus, part syringe, and extrudes from a vaginal/sphincteral slit in her armpit. She becomes a novel sexual combination – female/male/vampire. The underlying motif of unleashed sexual impulses causing personal/social destruction con-

36

nects with *Videodrome, Dead Ringers* and *Crash.* Slaying Sacred Cows: The army and National Guard have to battle the chaos unleashed by science; city officials and police are helpless. Secrets: Mindy is unaware of Rose's problem & Rose is unaware she is the carrier; finding out costs them their lives. Bizarre Organisations: The Keloid Clinic. Microcosm/ Macrocosm: Primal irrationality moves from high-rise interiors to city exteriors. Rose's plague infects Montreal, and obviously spreads wider still. Disease/Ageing/Death: The threat of this destructive epidemic is terrifying. People do not merely die; they first become insane and attack others in a zombie-like frenzy. Those not quarantined are shot in the streets under martial law. Fun for all in Cronenbergland!

Style: The brittle winter setting and cold, clean interiors emphasise the fragility of modern existence. Cronenberg always sites the most horrific events in the most commonplace locations (cinema, shopping mall, cattle barn, family home, clinic, police station, car, diner), destroying the illusion of social order and control. *Rabid* takes to the streets; the plague relocates from countryside to city. Things are always on the move, from Rose's ill-fated motorcycle ride to her body's removal in a dustcart. Characters hitch lifts, beg rides or restlessly head off on foot.

The smear of Lloyd's blood on the abstract print in Rose's room is a metaphysical digression on modern art's ability to reflect 'truth;' conversely, the barn sequence is composed in the style of an Old Master; country icons presented in an almost 'soft' formal tableau.

Trivia: Marilyn Chambers, porn star, was known as the Ivory Soap girl when she was young; a kind of Cronenbergian transformation in its own right. When Cronenberg's 80-year-old landlady found out she was in his film, she threw him out! He wanted Sissy Spacek for the role, but Ivan Reitman was convinced that Chambers would help sell the movie to the exploitation market. He was right.

Verdict: Cronenberg continues his philosophical enquiry into the effects of induced biological change on the individual and society. After the single bacterial culture of Starliner Towers, his microscope examines the wider human colony, through the elegiac waste of Rose's scared odyssey. *Rabid* is an underrated film, perhaps remaining in the shadow of future masterpieces. 3.5/5

"Family's like a gun. You point it in the wrong direction, you're going to kill somebody." – Matthew Slaughter (*Trust*, directed by Hal Hartley)

The Brood (1979)

Director/Screenplay David Cronenberg

Cast: Oliver Reed (Dr Hal Raglan), Samantha Eggar (Nola Carveth), Art Hindle (Frank Carveth), Cindy Hinds (Candice 'Candy' Carveth), Henry Beckman (Barton Kelly), Nuala Fitzgerald (Juliana Kelly), Susan Hogan (Ruth Mayer), Michael Magee (Inspector Mrazek), Joseph Shaw (Dr Desborough, Coroner), Gary McKeehan (Mike Trellan), Robert Silverman (Jan Hartog), Nicholas Campbell (Chris), Larry Solway (Resnikoff)

Credits: Production Companies Les Productions Mutuelles And Elgin International Productions, With The Participation Of The CFDC; Producer Claude Hèroux; Executive Producers Pierre David, Victor Solnicki; Cinematographer Mark Irwin; Editor Alan Collins; Music Howard Shore; Sound Bryan Day; Art Director Carol Spier; 1st Assistant Director John Board; Special Make-Up Jack Young, Dennis Pike; Special Effects Allan Kotter; 91 minutes, 35mm colour, 1.85:1

Story: At the Somafree Institute, Dr Hal Raglan humiliates his patient, Mike: "You're just a weak person. You must have got that from your mother. It probably would have been better for you if you had been born a girl." On the dimly-lit stage, Raglan demands a demonstration of anger, and Mike reveals angry red blotches covering his torso. The audience gasps. This is Psychoplasmics – the physical manifestation of mental rage.

Frank Carveth collects his daughter Candy from a 'Private Guest Room.' Candy wears a red coat with fur trim and hood. Bathing her, Frank finds bruises and scratches on her back. He drives to the Institute to confront Raglan and demands to see his wife Nola. Raglan refuses. Frank accuses Nola of abusing their daughter and says he will stop Candy's next visit. Raglan threatens legal action if Frank withholds a vital part of Nola's treatment. Frank's lawyer Al Resnikoff says Nola has the stronger legal position. Frank says he'll do what he has to. He takes Candy to her maternal grandmother Juliana, who seems highly strung.

Raglan (being Candice) asks Nola why she hurt her. Raglan/Candice says "Mummies don't hurt their own children." Nola sobs that they do; her own mother was "fucked up and bad." Raglan encourages her anger – "Go all the way through it, right to the end."

Juliana investigates a noise in the kitchen. Food, juice, glasses and dishes are thrown over the floor. She is bludgeoned by what appears to be a child in a hooded red coat with fur trim. As Candy watches, small claw-like hands leave bloodstains on the banisters. At his work, Frank is informed of Juliana's murder. Police psychologist Dr Birkin tells him to

encourage Candy to remember, a breakdown is possible if she doesn't –
"...these things tend to express themselves in one way or another."

Raglan speaks to Nola as her father. She is very angry – "You shouldn't have walked away when she hit me." Red welts appear on her forehead. At the airport, Frank and Candy meet Barton Kelly, Nola's father, who has come for his ex-wife's funeral. On Resnikoff's advice Frank visits Jan Hartog, an ex-Somafree patient taking legal action against Raglan. Uncovering a row of tumours on his neck, Hartog says bitterly "Raglan encouraged my body to revolt against me. And it did. I have a small revolution on my hands and I'm not putting it down very successfully."

At the Institute, a drunk Barton Kelly is furious when Raglan will not allow him to see Nola. Frank arrives late at Candy's school; her teacher Ruth Mayer sits with her. Candy invites Ruth to dinner. Barton telephones Frank from Juliana's house, saying he needs Frank's help to see Nola. Frank leaves Ruth baby-sitting, with a copy of *The Shape Of Rage*, Raglan's book on Psychoplasmics.

A small figure in a hooded red coat emerges from under Barton's bed and batters him with a pair of paperweights. Frank arrives and finds the body. The 'child' jumps him, but falls to the floor and expires, almost as if its batteries had run out. Ruth Mayer answers a phone call from Nola who goes berserk to find her there. Frank drives back, recalling the autopsy on the child-thing. Strange eyes. No sexual organs. No navel. The coroner's verdict is, "This creature has never really been born – at least, not the way human beings are born."

Raglan (as Ruth Mayer) speaks to Nola. Raglan/Ruth says Frank will divorce Nola and marry her. She screams to leave him alone. When Frank gets home Ruth leaves in a hurry. He finds Candy cowering in a corner of her room after a nightmare. He tells her the 'thing' is dead. Raglan reads about Barton Kelly's murder. Taking a gun from his desk, he instructs assistant Chris to get all the patients out of the Institute. Frank visits the hospital where Mike is now a fellow patient of Hartog's, and is told that Nola is the only patient at Somafree. Mike becomes angry about being dumped by his "daddy," his face one giant red sore.

Frank takes Candy to school. In Ruth Mayer's art class, two 'children' in pastel coats with hoods pick up wooden hammers and beat her mercilessly. Alerted by a boy's cries for help, Frank finds Ruth dead, and Candy gone.

Raglan wakes Nola. She relates a dream that Candy was coming back to her, and says she doesn't feel threatened by Ruth Mayer any more.

Candy is led along a snowy highway by the two creatures. Mike turns up on Frank's doorstep, raving about "...the disturbed kids in the workshed. The ones your wife's taking care of." Frank drives to Somafree. Raglan pulls a gun on him, saying they'll kill him if he tries to take Candy away from them: "Nola is not their surrogate mother, she's their real mother." They are the Brood – the parthenogenetic 'children' of Nola's rage. Frank must convince Nola that he wants her back. If he can do that, the Brood will be neutral and Raglan can take Candy. If not...

Nola rocks back and forth, wearing white robes and bathed in light. Frank says he wants to be with her. She throws back the robe, revealing external sacs on her abdomen. He recoils in horror. As Raglan wakes Candy the Brood stirs, sensing Nola's mounting anger. Nola tears open a sac, removing an 'infant' which she licks clean of blood, as an animal might. Frank's true feelings are obvious, and her rage erupts. In the attic, the Brood becomes active, leaping on Raglan and overwhelming him. Nola threatens to kill Candice rather than let Frank take her, and their attention turns to the petrified girl, who locks herself in another room. As they batter the door, Frank strangles Nola in order to save Candy. When Nola dies, all is silent.

As Frank drives home, Candy seems to have withdrawn into shock. Two raised lumps on her arm suggest like mother, like daughter...

Comment: Critical acclaim for *The Brood* was widespread. It is a move to a more personal kind of film-making, in every sense. By dissecting a family situation, fuelled by the angst of his own marital breakdown, Cronenberg proved himself capable of handling intimate character-based drama; albeit in his own inimitable, mutant fashion.

Themes: Cause And Effect: Nola is insane because she was abused by her own mother, or was she? Raglan's intense psychodramas provide the catalyst for the 'children' of her rage to kill those she feels threatened by, including her parents. The ability seems to re-emerge in Candy. Frankenstein Syndrome/The Absent (Or Mad) Scientist: Raglan, like Keloid and Hobbes, is brilliant in his field, but is undone by his failure to foresee the consequences of his own work. Mind/Body Schism: 'The sleep of reason produces monsters.' Psychoplasmics enables the mind to alter the body by externally realising its negative feelings. As Hartog's plight demonstrates, the paradox is that if the mind attacks the body, it also threatens its own existence. Altered States/Transformation: More Emergent evolution, as modern psychiatry releases a latent physical/mental ability. Postmodern/Existential Uncertainty: Does Raglan isolate Nola because she is psychoplasmics' star, or because his feelings for her run deeper? Is

Nola's control over her brood unconscious, or a manifestation of her all-too-conscious anger and jealousy? Was she beaten by her mother, or has she always possessed this rage? Are the lumps on Candy's skin caused by the trauma she undergoes, or heredity? Frank Carveth, another passive existential cipher, is powerless to influence anything until the very end, and then only negatively. Body/Sexual Horror: Childbirth becomes horrific when it is externalised, beyond normal reproductive functions. The image of Nola tearing at the birth-sac with her teeth is one that stays. Sexual attraction between Frank and Ruth threatens Nola's marriage, resulting in Ruth's murder. Hartog's cancerous wattles, Mike's lesions and Candy's lumps advance Cronenberg's singular vision. Slaying Sacred Cows: The family institution is shot down in flames. Psychiatry has sinister overtones. Secrets: Raglan keeps Nola's treatment secret. Nola and her mother recall their difficult past differently. Bizarre Organisations: The Somafree Institute Of Psychoplasmics. Microcosm/Macrocosm: Raglan's book on psychoplasmics is a best-seller. Nola's rage may manifest itself in many more adherents, perhaps unlocking the door to an epidemic. Disease/Ageing/Death: The spectre of death and disease is a Cronenberg mainstay. Is psychoplasmics a form of mental or physical illness? Faithless: Raglan's faith in his therapeutic methods is misguided. Cronenberg inventively reworks the Immaculate Conception.

Style: The brittle winter setting is even more alienating than in *Rabid*, evoking a soulless, oppressive mood. The colour scheme is darker than in the first two films, and richer. Brown/red is the central colour, especially in the wood-panelled Somafree outbuildings, and the lighting is more subdued. The houses are more lived in, the décor older-style and less modern, except for the clean architectural lines of the school and the Escher-like planes of the Institute. Nola's bare, natural wooden cabin provides a primitive birthplace for the Brood and is unlike anything before it. The lurid purple/pink glow bathing the autopsy scene is a very unCronenbergian stylistic device, included only to mask the deficiencies of the dummy. *The Brood*'s oppressive atmosphere, body-oriented colour scheme and character focus are a kind of dress rehearsal for *Videodrome*.

Trivia: Stephen Schiff commented "For my money, this is a horror-movie milestone, and the best work done in the genre since Kaufman's *Invasion Of The Body Snatchers*." Art Hindle starred in that movie opposite Brooke Adams, later to appear in *The Dead Zone*. Carol Spier's cover design for Raglan's book *The Shape Of Rage* (a clenched fist exploding into a primal scream) invokes the tortured imagery of artist Francis Bacon. The red-coated, hooded Brood 'children' recall the sinis-

41

ter figure of the murderous dwarf in Nic Roeg's superb psychological drama, *Don't Look Now*. The idea of creatures from the id attaining corporeal form is straight out of seminal 50's science fiction film *Forbidden Planet*, a point acknowledged by naming Candy's school the Krell school, after the mysterious race whose machines amplify thought into physical force. 'Somafree' refers to Aldous Huxley's dystopian novel *Brave New World*; Soma is a psychedelic drug used to control behaviour (and is the Greek word for 'body'). Philip K Dick's novel *The Man In The High Castle* features two main characters named Frank and Juliana.

Cronenberg was exorcising his own demons in *The Brood*. After being involved in a bitter divorce and custody battle for his daughter, the catharsis of the scene where Frank kills Nola is evident: "I can't tell you how satisfying that scene is," Cronenberg told Paul Sammon. "I wanted to strangle my ex-wife."

Verdict: The Brood, like many Cronenberg films, has an ethereal quality, a feeling of being caught in a languorous dreamstate. Its serene (though not slow) pace, and minute examination of the Carveth family closet builds a multilayered identity that draws you in. Cronenberg opens his heart (famously describing it, only half-jokingly, as "my version of *Kramer Vs Kramer*"), and the result is a poignant, thoughtful film that must have come as a surprise to many. 4/5

5. Man-Machine I: Roadkill

Fast Company (1979)

Director David Cronenberg; Screenplay Phil Savath, David Cronenberg, Courtney Smith; Story Alan Treen

Cast: William Smith (Lonnie Johnson), Claudia Jennings (Sammy), John Saxon (Phil Adamson), Nicholas Campbell (Billy Brooker), Cedric Smith (Gary Black), Judy Foster (Candy), George Buza (Meatball), Robert Haley (PJ), Don Francks (Elder)

Credits: Production Company Michael Lebowitz Inc (For Quadrant Films Ltd) With The Participation Of The CFDC; Producers Michael Lebowitz, Peter O'Brian, Courtney Smith; Executive Producer David M Perlmutter; Cinematographer Mark Irwin; Editor Ronald Sanders; Music Fred Mollin; Sound Bryan Day; Art Director Carol Spier; 91 minutes, 35mm colour, 1.85:1

Story: Ageing drag racing star Lonnie 'Lucky Man' Johnson makes engine refinements to his car, sponsored by oil company FastCo. On its first run it blows but Lonnie escapes unhurt, living up to his nickname. FastCo team boss Phil Adamson is not impressed, telling mechanic Elder the team can't afford to win if it breaks the budget. The real business is that the car remains competitive and helps sell FastCo product. In the Funny Car class, Lonnie's young protégé Billy 'The Kid' Brooker gives top dog Gary 'The Blacksmith' Black a close run.

On the road to Big Sky Lonnie calls his girlfriend Sammy, saying he misses her. When the FastCo rig blows a tyre, Black, jealous of FastCo's money and Lonnie's popularity, refuses to help. Adamson flies in his private plane with Candy Ellison, the pretty new FastCo girl. At the Big Sky meet, Adamson takes a backhander from the organiser: "The FastCo team sell tickets at this mosquito patch. If you don't want us to come..." He says the fans come to see Lonnie, so while the dragster is being repaired he will replace Billy in the Funny Car. Lonnie doesn't like it. Billy likes it less, blaming Lonnie's ego. Lonnie's first ever Funny Car run is against Black, who is angry at the driver switch, especially when he loses. Billy finds some compensation in the attractive presence of Candy.

En route to Spokane, Lonnie calls the dragster mechanic with a few ideas but is told Adamson cancelled the repair work. At the meet, Lonnie is less than complimentary on his FastCo TV spot. Adamson is incensed and phones the company to say he's bringing in Gary Black. Candy overhears the call, and when she refuses to screw the TV interviewer as damage limitation, Adamson fires her. He offers Black the FastCo ride. Candy and Billy get it on in Lonnie's trailer. Sammy visits and furiously assumes it's Lonnie in the bed, until he appears in the doorway. They make love and he talks of quitting. Adamson walks in without knocking, causing Lonnie to floor him. He says they're finished, but Lonnie assures him the car will race. Outside, Adamson gives Black's surly mechanic Meatball a job.

The Funny Car's engine blows, but Lonnie controls the situation using the cockpit safety gear. Billy angrily accuses Black of sabotage, but Lonnie intervenes on Black's behalf. In the pit, Adamson announces that Black is the new FastCo driver and the whole team is fired. Lonnie goes for him but is slugged with a tyre iron by Meatball.

Billy is despondent, but Lonnie insists they'll still race at Edmonton next weekend -they'll simply steal back the car! First though they have to find it. Billy and PJ visit the local motor show, and are amazed that Adamson has the car on display. That night, Billy and Candy create an amorous diversion for the security guard while Lonnie drives the car away. Working overtime, they get it in shape.

Edmonton. Night meet. Lonnie's surprise independent entry is announced. Adamson is worried that Black will be beaten, but Meatball says he will win as long as he is in the left lane. Black doesn't like it, but

Adamson tells him to shut up and drive. Lonnie gives an ecstatic Billy the ride. At the toss-up for lane choice, Billy wins and chooses left. Adamson ensures a last-minute change, and Billy's complaint is ignored. As the drivers wait on the start line, Black watches Meatball slope away, carrying two large cans of oil. At the green light, Billy gets a fast start but Black surges alongside and then swerves, seemingly trying to run him off the road. Black takes the lead, then cuts into Billy's lane and hits the oil that Meatball has poured on the track. His car explodes in a huge fireball. Billy can do nothing. He goes for Meatball at the side of the track, and in the struggle, Meatball's overalls catch fire. Billy uses his cockpit extinguisher to save his life.

The team arrives at the scene. Adamson panics and takes to his plane. As it taxies down the strip, Lonnie jumps in the Funny Car and hits the throttle. He catches up just as it takes off, clipping the end off a wing. Adamson fights for control but the plane dives into a parked FastCo oil truck, producing the second inferno of the night.

Later, the team members discuss the future. Lonnie promises he'll have new funding in place soon, but first he and Sammy are going to share some quality time. Billy and Candy like the sound of that, but Elder and PJ have a car to prepare.

Comment: Kim Newman wrote *"Fast Company*, ostensibly a film about drag racing, actually is a film about drag racing." For this reason, it is regarded as the only real anomaly in the Cronenberg Project. Although he has long had a passion for racing and fast cars, it stands apart from his (ab)normal celluloid obsessions. His 1976 TV film *The Italian Machine* is a bona fide attempt to integrate his love of fast machines into his unique filmic cosmology. *Fast Company*, however, is a film about drag racing.

Cronenberg said "It doesn't seem to fit with the rest of my work now, but it does. It has to fit; it's all coming from me... It was a good solid B-movie actioner, as they say, with some interesting elements." So, even Cronenberg can't make a convincing case for *why* it fits, it just does to him as its director. Because the rest of his *oeuvre* is so radical, challenging and downright bizarre, a "good solid B-movie actioner" about drag racing *can't* fit. It merits only a couple of pages in *Cronenberg On Cronenberg*, and in *The Shape Of Rage*, William Beard deliberately excludes it because of its "very great" difference from the rest of Cronenberg's work. This may be an inherent flaw of *auteur* criticism, but clichés are often true and the simple fact is that, compared to Cronenberg's other films, *Fast Company* is basically not that interesting.

Cronenberg has admitted many ideological clashes with his producer Michael Lebowitz ("I just thought they were doing their movie wrong"), and getting up at 5 am to do two hours of script rewriting and revisions before going on set. Not ideal conditions, though he pulled off similar situations on *Scanners* and *Videodrome*, as they were his material. *Fast Company* has enough action to keep the viewer involved, but the characters are cardboard stereotypes and the plot is hackneyed to say the least. The appalling MOR rock soundtrack gives the film an unfortunate *Dukes Of Hazzard* feel. Of chief interest for Cronenberg obsessives is his portrayal of the man/machine interface between high-performance machines and their drivers. Using documentary-style cockpit shots, the hooded drivers appear wired into the system, more metal than man. As for the film, it will probably be remembered as Claudia Jennings' last before her death, after making her name as the Queen of Exploitation in movies like *Truck Stop Women* and *The Great Texas Dynamite Chase*.

Verdict: Fast Company is for completists only, in the unlikely event they can track it down. 2/5

6. Mind Games I

"You're either in possession of a very new human ability, or a very old one" - Dr Sam Weizak (*The Dead Zone*)

Scanners (1980)

Director/Screenplay David Cronenberg
Cast: Stephen Lack (Cameron Vale), Michael Ironside (Darryl Revok), Patrick McGoohan (Dr Paul Ruth), Jennifer O'Neill (Kim Obrist), Lawrence Dane (Braedon Keller), Robert A Silverman (Benjamin Pierce), Adam Ludwig (Arno Crostic), Mavor Moore (Trevelyan), Fred Doederlein (Dieter Tautz), Victor Desy (Dr Gatineau), Victor Knight (Dr Frane), Louis Del Grande (Scanner)
Credits: Production Company Filmplan International Inc, With The Participation Of The CFDC; Producer Claude Hèroux; Executive Producers Pierre David, Victor Solnicki; Cinematographer Mark Irwin; Editor Ronald Sanders; Music Howard Shore; Sound Don Cohen; Art Director Carol Spier; Special Make-Up Stephan Dupuis, Chris Walas, Tom Schwartz; Special Make-Up Effects Consultant Dick Smith; Special Effects Gary Zeller; 103 minutes, 35mm colour, 1.85:1
Story: Scruffy derelict Cameron Vale rummages for leftovers in a mall café, watched by two disgusted women. Under Vale's gaze, one convulses and falls to the floor. Two men in raincoats give chase as he runs, firing a dart into his hand. He wakes strapped to a bed in a warehouse. Dr Paul Ruth tells him he is a derelict because he's a "scanner." Ruth ushers in a group of people whose voices grow in volume but their

lips do not move. Vale thrashes on the bed. Ruth administers an injection and the voices fade away.

In a ConSec lecture theatre an audience watches a demonstration of "scanning." A volunteer is asked to think of something specific, which the demonstrator will scan his thoughts to discover. The scanner directs his focus but is soon in great pain, shaking in mounting agony until his head literally explodes. Panic erupts. Security men lead the volunteer away at gunpoint. Dr Gatineau is told to administer a shot of "ephemerol," but injects his own hand instead. As the volunteer is driven to "the factory" a second security car suddenly swerves into a wall and explodes. The lead car stops to help. The man smiles as the chief of security shoots his two men and then himself.

Chairman Trevelyan addresses the board: "Last night, we at ConSec chose to reveal to the outside world our work with those telepathic curiosities known as 'Scanners.' The result – six corpses and a substantial loss in credibility for our organisation." New Director Of Security Braedon Keller wants the scanner program shut down. Ruth points out the man responsible is a scanner. His own scanners have all been lost to a powerful underground organisation led by the same man – Darryl Revok. He proposes infiltrating the organisation. Keller scoffs, but Ruth has a "very special" new scanner.

Ruth shows Vale a film of a younger Revok in a psychiatric institute, a hole drilled in his forehead. Revok says he did it to "let the people out." In a metro station Keller informs an unseen man about Vale.

Ruth stages a test. Vale makes Yoga master Dieter Tautz's heart beat faster, despite his efforts to retain control. In agony, he begs Vale to stop. Ruth is astonished by Vale's power. His next task is to find artist Benjamin Pierce, a possible link to Revok's underground. Vale makes gallery owner Arno Crostic an offer for one of Pierce's bizarre sculptures. When told it's impossible for him to meet the artist, he scans Crostic for Pierce's location, and is in turn scanned by a woman. When he turns around she is gone. At his rural workshop, Pierce is angered by Vale's arrival. Sitting inside a giant sculpted head, he refuses to answer questions. Four assassins burst in and open fire. Vale's scan flings them across the studio. The dying Pierce's thoughts give a name: "Kim Obrist."

Vale finds Kim, who is the woman from the gallery, but Revok has staked out her house. As her group sits in a circle, minds linked, two assassins start blasting before the scan throws them into a wall and they burst into flames. The survivors make their getaway in an old bus, but it is ambushed and ploughs into a record shop. An assassin follows, only to be paralysed by Vale's scan, which searches for something that will lead them to Revok. The man produces a vial with a 'Biocarbon Amalgamate' logo.

Biocarbon Amalgamate building. In the sterile environment, workers wear white fallout suits. One is Vale, watching as Revok directs operations. A computer shows a delivery of ephemerol. Access to the program, called 'Ripe,' is limited to ConSec terminals only.

Vale calls Ruth, saying he's bringing in an informant from Revok's group. At the metro station, Revok instructs Keller to kill Ruth if he discovers anything. Vale and Kim arrive at ConSec, and are injected with ephemerol. Keller takes Kim for interrogation. Vale protests, but Ruth confides their injections were harmless. Vale says Biocarbon Amalgamate manufactures ephemerol for Revok, and sends it out in tankers. The destinations are in the ConSec computer, meaning a traitor is working with Revok. Ruth tells Vale to access the Ripe program as he does not have computer clearance. Vale says neither does he. "No, but you do have a nervous system – and so does a computer."

Keller knows Kim is not from Revok's group. He pulls his gun but is overpowered by her scan. He sounds the alarm. Vale runs to find her, and Keller shoots Ruth. Vale and Kim use their scan to escape the guards.

Vale mentally downloads the Ripe program via a gas-station payphone. Keller is informed someone is accessing the program, and at gunpoint orders the technician to self-destruct the computer. This hurts Vale, but his wave of destructive energy surges down the line, causing an explosion which kills Keller. The overhead power lines set the gas station on fire and as it too explodes, he and Kim head for the nearest Doctor on the Ripe program list.

In Dr Frane's waiting room, Kim is scanned by a pregnant woman's unborn child. She is felled by a dart. Vale carries her outside, where Revok waits.

Vale awakes in Revok's office. Revok reveals that Paul Ruth was their father. He gave ephemerol to his pregnant wife, observing the side effects in his own children. Revok wants them to lead the "whole generation of scanner soldiers just a few months away from being born." Vale refuses and strikes Revok, who launches a ferocious mental assault. Vale loses the battle as Revok's ravaging scan causes his body to bleed, corrode and burn. His eyes seem calm until they are blown out. Revok summons a final intense burst.

Kim awakes and finds Vale's charred corpse, but senses... "Cameron?" In the corner of the room a figure huddles under a coat, which he throws off to reveal Revok's face now has Vale's eyes. "It's me, Kim. Cameron. I'm here. We've won. We've won..."

Comment: Scanners is a different kind of film for Cronenberg, one to which I'd like to see him return sometime. Although there are superb moments of body horror, the emphasis is on the mind and its latent capabilities. The ending, while not conclusively positive, is certainly more upbeat than before, and the film manages to retain the individual stamp that makes his work so unique and compelling.

Themes: Cause And Effect: Scanning ability is a side effect of the tranquilliser Ephemerol. Frankenstein Syndrome/The Absent (Or Mad) Scientist: Once more, a man of science reaps what he sowed. Ruth discovered telepathic side effects in his children and entered into an ill-fated Faustian pact with ConSec. Mind/Body Schism: Ruth tells Vale "Telepathy is not mind-reading. It is the direct linking of two nervous systems, separated by space." Scanning ability confers power over the physical as well as the mental (the film's tagline was 'Their thoughts can kill'). Altered States/Transformation: Scanners are a by-product of science. Their talent can be a curse, potentially causing severe psychological problems, or in Vale's case, dereliction. The new generation of scanners about to be born signals a wider evolutionary leap. Postmodern/ Existential Uncertainty: Although it may not at first appear so, *Scanners'* ending is ambiguous. Vale may think he has "won," but is Revok vanquished or merely dormant? Do other insane megalomaniacs await among the new-born scanner Brood? If 237 scanners cannot work together, what hope is there for a generation? ('...the centre cannot hold; mere anarchy is loosed upon the world.') The postmodern fragmented-head motif is again present; Pierce's broken-head sculpture becomes a literal as well as metaphorical environment. Tapping his head, he says "My art keeps me sane," which of course confirms his insanity. Ephemerol - the very name connotes transience and disposability. Body/ Sexual Horror: No sex in *The Brood*, nor *Scanners*. The nearest it gets is that scanners are an unforeseen side effect of a pregnancy drug (a Thalidomide for the mind?) Plenty of body horror though, in the infamous exploding head scene, and the gruesome destruction of Vale's body. Interesting that the man responsible for the 'birth' of the scanners is given a woman's name. Slaying Sacred Cows: Science gets it again. Corporate greed. Fatherly responsibility. Another dysfunctional family for the bonfire. Secrets: Paul Ruth conceals the legacy of his drug, uses his wife as a guinea pig, sells out and is revealed as Darth Vader to Vale's Luke Skywalker. Revok hides his programme to create new scanners. Vale's secret is his past, which even he is not aware of until the end (so how did he learn to drive, or use a computer? Why does he have no childhood memories? Or simply scan Ruth's mind?) Keller is in covert collaboration with Revok. Bizarre Organisations: ConSec, Biocarbon Amalgamate. Microcosm/Macrocosm: Ruth's invention led to the creation of first two, then 237 scanners. Revok's Ripe programme leads to thousands more. Disease/Ageing/Death: Death is never far away, most of the cast get theirs. Scanning talent is a kind of disease if you can't deal with it. Faithless: There may not be life after death, but there's certainly a spiritual house move. Vale strikes a serene, Christ-like pose as his body burns and his mind is 'reborn' in Revok's body. Having done it once, he can presumably do it again. The sins of the father are visited upon his sons, and others – by extension, all scanners are Ruth's 'children.'

Style: Scanners has all the attributes of a genre thriller. It rattles along at a frantic pace, has a complex plot, (far too complex to sustain credibility) involving dangerous corporations, underground groups, double agents, car chases, explosions and, er, modern art. Dehumanising architecture is again associated with science in the ConSec and Biocarbon Amalgamate buildings. Ruth is ostracised from the scientific fold in his 'factory' – a brick warehouse. Bad guy/good guy is emphasised by costume. Vale's all-white clothing contrasts with Ruth's all-black and Revok's black/white shirt/waistcoat/tie (business wear as evil uniform? The office is the arena for the final battle). Physical effects of scanning vary from nosebleeds to exploding skulls. Red blood against a pale background is a motif repeated from *Shivers* and *The Brood*. Cronenberg's quirky dialogue is given full rein; his odd sense of humour very much evident (when Vale tries to gain Pierce's confidence by saying "I'm one of you." The puzzled reply is "You're one of *me*?") The lively, Mozart feel of the score segues into an intense, melancholy theme that Howard Shore has never bettered.

Trivia: The asylum holding young Revok is called The Crane Institute – *Psycho*, anyone? The synthesised scan tone is reminiscent of *Forbidden Planet*, in which shrill, electronic textures also signal rising mental pressure. The term 'Scanner' may refer to Philip K Dick's novel *A Scanner Darkly*, although Dick uses the term differently. *Scanners* prompted writer/director John Carpenter to remark that Cronenberg was better than the rest of his contemporaries put together.

Cronenberg cast Stephen Lack primarily because of his large, limpid eyes, and his performance was roundly slated. Comparatively, Michael Ironside makes a fabulously compelling villain. A number of appalling 'sequels' have been made, franchising the *Scanners* name. Avoid.

Verdict: It is impossible for me to be objective about this film. On first viewing, it exploded my head too. Sure, there are plot holes and inconsistencies, poor performances and laughable moments, but I still adore it. The siblings' mental battle in their psychic gymnasium is one of the great tour de force sequences of science fiction cinema, augmented by Shore's incredible music. With zero preparation time and a skeletal script, it's a miracle it hangs together as well as it does. 4.5/5

"I'm feeling a little disconnected from my real life"
– Ted Pikul *(eXistenZ)*

Videodrome (1982)

Director/Screenplay David Cronenberg

Cast: James Woods (Max Renn), Sonja Smits (Bianca O'Blivion), Deborah Harry (Nicki Brand), Peter Dvorsky (Harlan), Les Carlson (Barry Convex), Jack Creley (Brian O'Blivion), Lynne Gorman (Masha), Julie Khaner (Bridey), Rainer Schwartz (Moses), David Bolt (Raphael), Lally Cadeau (Rena King)

Credits: Production Company Filmplan International II Inc, With The Participation Of The CFDC; Producer Claude Hèroux; Executive Producers Pierre David, Victor Solnicki; Associate Producer Lawrence S Nesis; Cinematographer Mark Irwin; Editor Ronald Sanders; Music Howard Shore; Art Director Carol Spier; Sound Bryan Day; Creative Consultant Denise Di Novi; 1st Assistant Director John Board; Make-Up Design & Creation Rick Baker; Make-Up Artists Steve Johnson, Bill Sturgeon; Video Effects Michael Lennick; 87 minutes, 35mm colour, 1.85:1

Story: Max Renn, President of sleazy Toronto cable station Channel 83/Civic TV, is woken up by a video alarm call from his assistant Bridey. In a dingy hotel room, two Japanese businessmen from Hiroshima Video play him their latest soft-core porn opus, 'Samurai Dreams.' Later, his partners Moses and Raphael like it but Max is unimpressed: "I'm looking for something that'll break through, you know? Something – tough." His prayers are answered when technician/video pirate Harlan intercepts a scrambled broadcast, possibly from Malaysia: two hooded men torture a woman against a wall of reddish-brown wet clay. Intrigued, Max wants more.

He guests on Rena King's TV talk show, with C-RAM's radio agony aunt Nicki Brand and "media prophet" Professor Brian O'Blivion, who appears only on video. Max lives up to his controversial reputation by propositioning Nicki.

Harlan now has an hour of the 'tough' show, Videodrome. The time delay was a decoy; it is actually broadcast from Pittsburgh. Max visits C-RAM as Nicki's 'Emotional Rescue' show is on air. Afterwards in his apartment she looks for porno tapes, picking out Videodrome. He warns "It ain't exactly sex." She likes it. She asks him to cut her shoulder, and to "try a few things." Max does so, uneasily. As he pierces her ear, he hallucinates they are in Videodrome.

He meets Masha Borowski, whose soft-core porn toga saga 'Apollo and Dionysus' is just too tame. He brings up Videodrome. "It's just torture and murder. No plot, no characters. Very, very realistic. I think it's what's next." She responds, "Then God help us," but agrees to track it down for an agent's commission. Nicki tells Max she's going to Pittsburgh on assignment, where she'll audition for Videodrome. Furious, he says it's too rough even for her. She responds by defiantly burning her breast with a cigarette.

Masha warns Max off Videodrome: "It's not acting, it's real," but she has a name – Brian O'Blivion. Max goes to the Cathode Ray Mission, O'Blivion's soup kitchen for derelicts, with TVs in every cubicle. His daughter Bianca says her father sees no one. Max tells her to mention Videodrome and he will.

Bridey brings Max his wake-up cassette, plus another from O'Blivion's office. She says according to C-RAM Nicki Brand is on leave, not assignment. Max slaps her face hard and, shocked, apologises. As he ushers her out, she says he didn't hit her. When he picks up O'Blivion's tape, it pulses organically. O'Blivion's message informs Max his reality is "already half video-hallucination," as a hooded figure straps him into his chair and strangles him. Max is aghast. The hood is removed to reveal Nicki. Her lips fill the screen as she purrs "Come to me." Max leans close. Pulsing and undulating, the screen envelops his face.

At the Mission, Bianca O'Blivion is unsurprised about Max's hallucinations. They are a side effect of the Videodrome signal which induces a brain tumour in the viewer, and killed her father. Frantic, Max asks what he can do as he's also been exposed. She sends him away with an armful of tapes. As he watches, holding his gun, he scratches his stomach. A vagina-like slit opens, into which the gun disappears. On tape, O'Blivion says "...there is nothing real outside our perception of reality, is there?"

Max is called by Barry Convex, who wants to discuss Videodrome. In Convex's limo, his video introduction tells Max that once Videodrome hits the market, "things will never be the same again." He is taken to the downtown shop/office of 'Spectacular Optical,' who make "inexpensive glasses for the third world and missile-guidance systems for NATO." Convex produces a high-tech helmet to record Max's hallucinations, to find out why he seems to be functioning when none of the other "test subjects" has returned to "normality." Convex places the helmet on Max's head and leaves.

Max hallucinates himself in Videodrome with Nicki. As he whips an organic TV set, Nicki's image transforms into Masha. Max awakes in his own bed; Masha is dead by his side. He calls Harlan, who arrives with his camera but sees nothing in the bed to photograph. Totally wired, Max says they must watch last night's Videodrome broadcast, as he is on it. At the lab, Harlan reveals there never was a broadcast, only pre-recorded tapes, which he never watched. Convex enters. He says they chose Channel 83 for the first transmission of the Videodrome signal because of its sleazy content and audience; "Why would anybody watch a show like Videodrome?" Convex produces a pulsating tape and Max's stomach-slit opens to receive his program – "Kill your partners and give us Channel 83." Max pulls his gun from the slit and black metal tendrils extend into his hand.

Max shoots Moses and Raphael in the Channel 83 boardroom, his gun/hand now a single organic fusion. His next program is to kill Bianca O'Blivion. He breaks into the Mission, but hesitates as Bianca plays him Nicki Brand's death on Videodrome. A flesh-gun emerges from the TV and shoots him - a violent deprogramming. Bianca inserts her own tape. She tells him he is "the video word made flesh. Death to Videodrome. Long live the new flesh."

Harlan congratulates Max on his good work and changes his program. When Harlan withdraws his hand from Max's slit, he is horrified to see it has become a ticking organic grenade. The explosion blows a hole in the wall through which Max calmly steps. At the Spectacular Optical trade show, Convex introduces the new spring collection, the Medici range. Max approaches the stage and shoots Convex, whose body erupts in a sickening mass of tumours.

Max walks to the docks and takes refuge in a condemned vessel. He sits on a filthy mattress, watching a TV image of Nicki, who says "To become the new flesh, you first have to kill the old flesh." The TV image shows him raising the hand/gun to his temple. As he shoots, the TV explodes in a shower of offal. He stands and repeats the movement, closing his eyes. "Long live the new flesh."

Comment: Videodrome is perhaps the definitive statement of Cronenberg's cosmology. An incredibly complex, labyrinthine puzzle, its myriad layers and connections merit a book in their own right. An analysis of this length can merely cut a small nick with a Swiss army knife.

Themes: Cause And Effect: Max's unhealthy fascination with Videodrome leads to his corruption by it. Because of Civic TV's sex n' violence content, Spec Op's corporate reactionaries target it to broadcast the deadly signal. Frankenstein Syndrome/The Absent (Or Mad) Scientist: O'Blivion meets his end as a result of his own creation, and although 'absent,' appears in the narrative via video technology. Mind/Body Schism: The uncontrolled spiral of Max's mind becomes the very fabric of the film. On a representative level, Bianca is the cool, intellectual woman (mind) and Nicki is the sexual, aggressive woman (body). O'Blivion existed in a mental realm of ideas; Convex exists in a physical world of power and control. Altered States/Transformation: What does Max become? Cronenberg emphasises narrative subjectivity; *"Videodrome* really has to do with personal morality and personal darkness. It has to do with a person coming into contact with certain very dark, scary parts of himself and what happens to him while confronting them." Postmodern/Existential Uncertainty: *Videodrome* is the ultimate fragmented postmodernist narrative. Objectivity is absent because Max is the absolute focus. We only 'know' what Max knows. Reality cannot be trusted because perception cannot be trusted – very PhilDickian. To what extent are Max's hallucinations 'real'? After his exposure to the Videodrome signal, does the narrative continue in his mind? If not, when the Accumicon helmet is placed on his head and we never see it removed, does the narrative continue in his mind? If not, then does he attain a new plane of existence and become "the new flesh," or commit pointless suicide? Is it paranoia, or are they really out to get him? No answers, only questions. Through Max's (and therefore our) flawed senses, *Videodrome* deconstructs the Grand Narrative of visual media, reducing it to a succession of hallucinatory surfaces reflecting elusive, shifting realities. Body/Sexual Horror: Max's abdominal slit (after Rose's 'penis' comes Max's 'vagina'); the penile hand/gun; the hand/grenade; body piercing; and (Nicki) branding; Convex's tumours; organic, pulsing TVs and videotapes; S & M, torture and mutilation – your average Cronenberg popcorn movie. Slaying Sacred Cows: Cronenberg's films tear down social order, but also display a reactionary distaste towards the mechanisms by which this is accomplished (in this case, sleazy cable TV). This contradiction has been criticised, but he takes no concrete position, merely invites debate ("I'm very balanced. I'm cursed with balance, which is to say I immediately see all sides to a story"). Secrets: Max's innermost secrets are the substance of the text. Bizarre Organisations: Spectacular Optical, Hiroshima Video, Cathode Ray Mission. Microcosm/Macrocosm: The individual is at the mercy of systems and groups. Max is manipulated by Bianca as much as by Convex; both use him as a dehumanised assassin, literally 'fucking him' via his vaginal slit. The Videodrome signal is tested on the few before being unleashed on the many. Disease/Ageing/Death: "TV gives you cancer!" (Hartley's *Trust* again.) The medium may be the message, but its subsignal (subtext) is also the disease. Faithless: Faith is a shield against awkward questions. Max has ultimate faith that by killing his old flesh he'll become the new flesh (the case for religion as mental illness?) The Cathode Ray Mission's aim is to patch social derelicts back into the world's mixing board by means of television, which for O'Blivion has assumed a greater status than reality. (Who else except Cronenberg would advance theories like these, even tongue-in-cheek, never mind get away with it?)

Style: Cronenberg's ability to unite mise en scène and narrative to create a powerful emotional bomb is special; as is his cool, distanced manner when dealing with the most out-there material. "I'm allowing you to watch tapes of my dreams, fantasies, nightmares, with all the complexity that entails. I often think that my films really work on dream logic. I like narrative that *seems* to make sense, and then suddenly, in a way, it doesn't..."

The rich, orange/brown colour scheme is highly body-conscious and connotes danger. It is constantly repeated; in Videodrome, the condemned vessel, the organic TV sets, 'Samurai Dreams,' Nicki's striking red dress that prompts Max's interest, her video image's hair, the Accumicon helmet's glow. Red and black contrasts abound. Repetition of colours and objects evokes mood. The 'special' colours dominate the drab, gloomy 'normal' world of neutral greys and pastels. Many 'disposable' objects from earlier scenes reappear in Max's hallucinations. The accessories inside the ship subliminally précis earlier episodes; the chain, the rope and the iron bed frame recall the Videodrome set, the mattress and the cigarettes evoke Nicki and sex, the green bottle from the hotel room represents the soft-core of 'Samurai <u>Dreams</u>' and the road not taken (Max's life flashing before his eyes?) Max's apartment is full of TV metaphors: glass panels like multiple screens; the bluish hue of the lighting and horizontal blinds suggesting scan lines. The full list is far greater, encompassing texture, lighting and camera movement in a phenomenally intricate matrix.

54

The clutter of the décor illustrates Max's disordered mindset. Downbeat locations strip away the veneer of social respectability and order so apparent before, and add to the oppressive dread of Max's downward spiral. Bianca even compares him to a derelict. (Cameron Vale goes from derelict to messiah; Max Renn passes through dereliction before either blowing his brains out or transcending the flesh.) Again, doors are used to reveal and conceal, and as metaphoric levels for Max's journey. The final door he passes through bears the legend 'Condemned.'

Trivia: Extra plot twists in various script drafts (some filmed) are intriguing. While at the Mission to kill Bianca, Max discovers Nicki - either the women are business partners, or Max's fevered psyche has somehow merged them. Nicki shows Max a flesh-TV image of Bianca, wearing the seductive red dress. Bianca tells him "We can't stop where you are now... stuck in the middle. Not us. Not Bianca, Max and Nicki." Another sequence involved a flesh-TV emerging from Max's bathtub (recalling *From The Drain* and *Shivers*). Max originally viewed Nicki's death on Videodrome in the lab, and the Accumicon helmet had its own history; developed for military night vision, a side effect caused soldiers to project their own hallucinations. The idea was scrapped when Cronenberg realised its glow would render it useless for night exercises! Two alternative versions of the end were discarded. In one, after Max shoots himself, we see him with Nicki in Videodrome, blissfully happy. In the other, Max, Nicki and Bianca are in Videodrome, exploring each other's abdominal/vaginal slits, from which emerge novel sex organs, before they all morph together into one. This echoes the idea of 'omnisexuality' in *Stereo*, the strange new organs in *Crimes Of The Future* and the orgiastic excesses of *Shivers*.

The character of Brian O'Blivion is humorously modelled on Canadian 'media prophet' Marshall McLuhan, famous for cryptic statements like "The medium is the message," "TV is the extension of the tactile sense" and "The viewer is the screen."

Verdict: Truly visionary. Cronenberg says "...I was really breaking some new ground; I hadn't seen anything like it myself." Special mention goes to Howard Shore's electronic score, realised on the then state-of-the-art Synclavier synthesizer. Sensual, unsettling, profound; a perfect compliment to the film's provocative images and knife-edge melancholia. *Videodrome* is Cronenberg's masterpiece, pure and simple. One of the best films of the 80s and possibly the strongest emotional devastation I've experienced in a cinema. 5/5

"I see too deep and too much" – (*L'Enfer* by Henri Barbusse)

The Dead Zone (1983)

Director David Cronenberg; Screenplay Jeffrey Boam; Novel Stephen King
Cast: Christopher Walken (Johnny Smith), Brooke Adams (Sarah Bracknell), Martin Sheen (Greg Stillson), Sean Sullivan (Herb Smith), Jackie Burroughs (Vera Smith), Herbert Lom (Dr Sam Weizak), Tom Skerritt (Bannerman), Anthony Zerbe (Roger Stuart), Nicholas Campbell (Frank Dodd), Geza Kovacs (Sonny Elliman), Colleen Dewhurst (Henrietta Dodd), Peter Dvorsky (Dardis), Barry Flatman (Walt), Simon Craig (Chris Stuart), Les Carlson (Brenner), Roberta Weiss (Alma Frechette)

Credits: Production Company Dead Zone Productions In Association With Lorimar Productions Inc; Producer Debra Hill; Executive Producer Dino De Laurentiis; Associate Producer Jeffrey Boam; Cinematographer Mark Irwin; Editor Ronald Sanders; Music Michael Kamen; Sound Bryan Day; Production Designer Carol Spier; 1st Assistant Director John Board; Special Effects Coordinator Jon G Belyeu; Special Effects Mark Molin, Michael Kavanagh, Derek Howard, Clark Johnson; Video & Electronic Effects Michael Lennick; Stunt Coordinator Dick Warlock; 100 minutes, 35mm colour, 1.85:1

Story: After class, Maine schoolteacher Johnny Smith takes sweetheart Sarah to an amusement park. On the roller coaster he suffers a bad headache. Sarah invites him to stay, but he declines ("Some things are worth waiting for"). As he drives home, a tanker jackknifes in front of him and he ploughs into it. He awakes in the Weizak Clinic. His parents are shown in. He has been in a coma for five years, and Sarah has married another man. He is inconsolable.

As a nurse mops his brow, he seizes her hand. He has a super-real vision of being trapped in a screaming girl's blazing bedroom. He tells the nurse, "Amy needs your help." Amy is her daughter's name. She rushes home to find her house in flames, but her daughter safe.

When told he will walk again, John gratefully takes Weizak's hand and is jolted by another vision. Wartime. Burning buildings, advancing tanks. A protesting young boy is lifted onto a horse-drawn cart, leaving his mother behind. John tells Sam his mother survived. Weizak says it's impossible, but John knows her name and address. Weizak checks; it's true, but he can't bring himself to speak to his mother. He tells John, "You're either in possession of a very new human ability – or a very old one."

John has a visitor - Sarah. Catching his stare, she asks him not to look at her that way. He can't help it – for her it's been five years, but for him it's the next day. She says she has a son, Denny. He takes it well. She tells him his power of "second sight" is the talk of the town. Against Weizak's advice, he gives a press conference to defuse the situation. Cynical TV reporter Dardis demands a demonstration. Aware he is being mocked, John takes his hand – "You wanna know why your sister killed herself?" Dardis calls him a freak. John's distressed parents watch on TV, and his mother collapses. At the hospital, John holds her hand as she dies.

John moves in with his father. Sheriff Bannerman pays a visit to ask for his help to catch the 'Castle Rock killer.' John refuses. When told he should use the gift he's been blessed with, John is furious. He sees it as a curse. Sarah brings her son over when Herb is out. She puts Denny to bed and says, "Haven't we waited long enough?" They finally make love.

After watching a TV programme about the killer, John decides to help. Bannerman and Officer Dodd take him to the scene of the last murder, but he gets nothing. Bannerman is called to another murder. In the park bandstand is a woman's frozen corpse. Dodd identifies her as local waitress Alma Frechette. John takes her hand and instantly 'sees' a man calling to her from the bandstand. "She knows him." John watches, powerless, as she is killed with a pair of scissors. The man reveals his face: Dodd. Bannerman calls him, but he has left in the car. At Dodd's house, as his mother tries to stop John entering, he realises she knew all along. She calls him a devil, sent from hell. In the bathroom, Dodd impales his mouth on the scissors. His mother takes his gun and shoots John, forcing Bannerman to kill her.

John moves out of town. The bullet injury has healed but the headaches are getting worse. He takes private tutoring jobs, and is persuaded by millionaire Roger Stuart to teach his introverted son Chris. John arrives at Stuart's mansion as loud, abrasive politician Greg Stillson is leaving. John and Chris get on well, to Stuart's relief. Later, he and John watch TV coverage of Stillson's campaign. Stuart says Stillson is popular, and dangerous. In local newspaper editor Brenner's office, Stillson and his sidekick Sonny demand he retract an anti-Stillson editorial in the next edition. Producing photographs of Brenner with a young woman, they threaten to "take his head off" if he doesn't.

A tutorial session is interrupted by a Stillson campaigner at the door. A woman brings him a brochure - Sarah. The man is her husband Walt. After an uneasy introduction, they leave and John breaks down. As Chris hugs him, John has a vision of kids in hockey uniforms falling through ice. One of them is Chris. John goes to Stuart and insists he call off the kids' ice hockey practise, or they'll drown. Stuart fires him despite Chris' pleas. At a news-stand, John reads a headline about two boys drowning in a skating accident. He calls Stuart's house, hanging up in relief when Chris answers.

Stillson's next rally takes place opposite John's house. Looking for Sarah, John finds himself in Stillson's path. As they shake hands, another vision strikes: President Stillson orders a general to co-authorise the missile launch that will cause nuclear Armageddon. Stillson is shaken and Sonny pushes John away.

Asked by John if he could go back in time knowing what he knows now, would he kill Hitler, Weizak answers affirmatively. He thinks the "dead zone" in John's visions means that as well as seeing the future, he can also change it.

John packs up his rifle and takes a bus. He breaks into the hall where Stillson will appear next day and lies in wait. As the hall fills, Stillson arrives and invites Sarah and Denny onto the stage. On the balcony, John rises and takes aim. Sarah screams his name, and he misses. Panicked, Stillson snatches Denny from Sarah. John hesitates, and is shot by Sonny. He plummets to the floor. A youth photographs it all. Stillson grabs John, to find out who sent him. John's final vision is a Newsweek cover of Stillson using Denny as a shield; the headline 'No Future For Stillson.' Stillson takes a gun and commits suicide. John tells him "It's over. You're finished." Stillson goes after the youth who took the pictures. John tells Sarah he loves her and dies, his mission accomplished.

Comment: Cronenberg proved he could direct other people's scripts without losing the overwhelming emotional impact he had been building. *The Brood, Scanners* and *Videodrome* all leave you in an enraptured inertia, a sense of being mentally stunned and bodily weak. Driven by a wonderful performance from Walken, *The Dead Zone* has a similar effect – diluted for the mass market, but a rare and valuable talent for a film-maker to possess.

Themes: Cause And Effect: The film associates John's headaches and eventual psychic ability with the accident and coma (in the novel, they are caused by an ice-skating accident aged six). Frankenstein Syndrome/ The Absent (Or Mad) Scientist: Cronenberg has made his own auteurist case for God to be considered as the absent scientist of *The Dead Zone*, with John as his failed experiment. Mind/Body Schism: John has no control over his faculty to predict the future; his visions are akin to seizures, which slowly kill his body. Altered States/Transformation: John is transformed by forces beyond his control into another state of being, in which he can see (crimes of) the future, resulting in his own destruction. Typical Cronenbergian scenario, isn't it? Perhaps that's why he was so keen.

Postmodern/Existential Uncertainty: Does John Smith (Joe Average) really see the future? His story about Weizak's mother checks out, as does his discovery of Dodd's alter ego, and the fire at the nurse's house. However, Chris Stuart might not have died had he played ice hockey, and there's no objective proof of Stillson's destiny to become President and destroy the world. If John's visions are fallible, then he has followed in Max Renn's footsteps and become an Outsider, driven over the edge of the abyss by his own flawed senses. Body/Sexual Horror: Comparatively, *The Dead Zone* is a model of restraint. The one grisly moment, Dodd's suicide by scissors, is small potatoes when set against Cronenberg's usual raw meat. Slaying Sacred Cows: Police (they cannot detect the killer without John's assistance), true love, politicians. Secrets: Sarah keeps the belated consummation of her relationship with John a secret from Walt. Stillson's true nature is only brought to public attention by John's talent. Dodd's secret alter ego is the Castle Rock killer, and his mother hides her knowledge of his actions. Bizarre Organisations: The Weizak Clinic (not really bizarre, but another addition to the list of Cronenberg clinics). Microcosm/Macrocosm: What begins as personal tragedy is exposed by press interest, and ends as a national event, hitting the cover of Newsweek. Disease/Ageing/Death: John's mental power is more disease than blessing, (much like scanning ability) and ages him, bringing him closer to death. Faithless: John's mother is a religious woman who becomes evangelistically unbalanced following his coma. He says "God's been a real sport to me!" He may be a religious agent, doing God's dirty work for Him, or a deluded slave to a false reality. Renn, Brundle, Vaughan, Gallimard, the Mantle twins... what Cronenberg loves about his Outsiders is that "...they cannot turn the mind off; and the mind undercuts, interprets, puts into context. To allow themselves to go totally into the emotional reality of what's happening to them is to be destroyed completely."

Style: Precise, no-nonsense direction propels the film and tells the story without waste. Cronenberg is always at home as a film-maker, literally as well as creatively, always shooting in and around Toronto. He is also at home in a winter landscape, and the picturesque location of Niagara-On-The-Lake (doubling for King's trademark New England settings) is used to good effect. This is not the brittle, blanched coldness of *Rabid, The Brood* or *Videodrome*. The location reflects the humanity of the story and although the snow and bright lighting possess a lonely quality, it is used as a counterpoint to those films' mood of helpless despair. Carol Spier's production design is a homage to New England artist Norman Rockwell. His *Saturday Evening Post* covers helped define the myth of happy, homely mid-America. The posters for Stillson's campaign are in the style of his portraits of Eisenhower.

Trivia: Jeffrey Boam completed his first draft script the day Reagan was elected President! Cronenberg actually *rejects* a brain tumour, which in the novel is a consequence of John's visions. Martin Sheen's son Ramon Estevez (also Sheen's real name) is the youth who photographs Stillson's cowardice. Cronenberg rejected Boam's original De Palma-esque ending. In it, the Castle Rock killer is jailed but escapes and goes after John. After being shot by Sonny, John is taken to hospital. He whispers "Garage" to his father. Herb walks Sarah to the basement parking garage, where Dodd lurks. Dodd hacks Sarah with a knife, but it becomes apparent that this is John's vision of her death when we cut to Herb, pondering the significance of John's warning. Back in the garage, the killer is about to strike when Herb beats him unconscious with John's walking stick. No, I don't like it either.

The idea that Stillson snatches Denny came from a chance remark by Walken. Stephen King liked the film a lot, but he was unhappy with that scene. Originally, John fired at Stillson anyway, and King argued this made him seem prepared to risk Denny's life. Cronenberg agreed, and simply re-edited the shots in a different order. He also deleted the three-minute prologue showing young John's ice hockey accident, because he felt it was cleaner to link the visions to the coma.

Like *Scanners* and *Videodrome*, the film benefits from an excellent score, this time by Michael Kamen. Lush, poignant, haunting and powerful, it was composed in three weeks after Michel Legrand pulled out.

Verdict: Cronenberg's Hollywood movie, in the very best sense of the term. A slick, engaging narrative with a tragic love affair at its core. ("It's a tear-jerker.") Although toned down from his preceding work, it remains a moving, multifaceted accomplishment. 4/5

7. Altered States

"The reshaping of the human body by modern technology"
– Vaughan (Crash)

The Fly (1986)

Director David Cronenberg; Screenplay David Cronenberg, Charles Edward Pogue; Original Story George Langelaan
Cast: Jeff Goldblum (Seth Brundle), Geena Davis (Veronica Quaife), John Getz (Stathis Borans), Joy Boushel (Tawny), Les Carlson (Dr Cheevers), George Chuvalo (Marky), David Cronenberg (Gynaecologist), Carol Lazare (Nurse)

Credits: Production Company Brooksfilms; Executive Producers Marc-Ami Boyman, Kip Ohman; Producer Stuart Cornfeld; Cinematographer Mark Irwin; Editor Ronald Sanders; Music Howard Shore; Sound Bryan Day; Production Designer Carol Spier; Creature Creation & Design Chris Walas Inc; Costume Designer Denise Cronenberg (David's sister); 92 minutes, 35mm colour, 1.85:1

Story: At a Bartok Science Industries party, brilliant but eccentric young scientist Seth Brundle pitches his work to attractive journalist Veronica Quaife as "...something that will change the world and human life as we know it." Despite her scepticism, she accompanies him to his austere, warehouse-like lab. She examines his project hardware, remarking "designer phone booths." He calls them "telepods," and asks for an object of hers for a demonstration. She removes a stocking, which to her astonishment he then teleports from one pod to the other. He grins like a kid showing off a toy.

She changes her walkman tape. He forbids her to write about what she's seen. She retorts that Particle Magazine sent her to the party to find a story, and he can't stop her. However, Particle editor and her ex-lover Stathis Borans is certain that Brundle has used an old nightclub trick to con her. Brundle follows her to Borans' office and invites her for a cheeseburger. He proposes that she write up his project as a book, which will end with the solution to the problem of teleporting animate matter, using himself as the final subject.

In his lab she videotapes a teleportation experiment on a baboon. It goes horribly wrong and the animal is reintegrated inside-out. Brundle is upset and depressed; "It can't deal with the flesh." She stays with him and they make love. After a chance remark of hers, Brundle tries an experiment with steak. The normal half is fine, but the teleported half tastes wrong, "synthetic." He announces that he must make the computer "crazy about the flesh." She drives away, watched by Borans, who confronts her next day in a clothes store, and is angrily dismissed.

After some computer refinements, Brundle's next attempt to teleport a baboon appears successful. He breaks out champagne and orders Chinese, but she finds an unopened envelope from the desk of Stathis Borans. It contains a mock-up Particle Magazine cover of Brundle with the headline 'The Father Of Teleportation.' She leaves to confront Borans without giving a reason. Brundle takes this the wrong way and gets jealously drunk. As he watches the baboon trying to swat a fly he's sure it's alright, and on impulse teleports himself. Unaware that the fly is now also in the telepod...

Later that night, after promising to keep Borans informed as her editor but insisting on control of the story, Veronica returns. She awakes to find Brundle going through an incredible gymnastic routine. He is on energy overdrive, hyperactive, gorging on sugar and chocolate. During sex she can't last his pace. She removes coarse hairs from his back. He feels so supercharged that he insists she go through the telepod to feel the same. She refuses, telling him something went wrong. Enraged, he accuses her of being "afraid to dive into the plasma pool," and storms out to find someone who can keep up with him.

In a sleazy bar, he challenges macho man Marky to arm-wrestle; the stake is his 'girlfriend' Tawny for the night, or $100. Marky thinks it's easy money, but Brundle breaks his arm and walks out with her. He takes her back to the lab and teleports again before fucking her. Afterwards, he drags her to the pod but Veronica arrives and tells her "Be afraid. Be very afraid." The analysis of the hairs from his back shows they're not human, but insect. He throws her out, but he knows something is happening to him. His fingers are full of pustules and his face is liquefying.

He examines computer data relating to his teleportation, and finds that instead of one subject there were two; a graphic shows the second subject was a fly. He types 'What happened to fly? Assimilation?' To his horror, it answers in the negative: Brundle and fly have been fused at the molecular-genetic level. Brundlefly.

Four weeks later he calls Veronica. He is literally falling apart, perhaps due to "a bizarre form of cancer." She can't help him and, deeply upset, goes to Borans for advice. He asks to see Brundle for himself. When she plays a tape of Brundle vomiting digestive juices over his food before ingesting it, as a fly does, he can't believe it. However, a more immediate problem is that she is pregnant - with Brundle's child.

Borans takes her to have it terminated. In the operating room, the gynaecologist pulls out a large, long, wriggling worm-like thing... with a jolt, she awakes from her nightmare. When she next visits Brundle he is walking on the ceiling, in an advanced stage of transformation. He tells her the insect is taking over and if she stays he'll hurt her. She is devastated, and outside screams at Borans to get her an immediate abortion, unaware they are being watched from the roof. Borans takes her to Dr Cheevers, but Brundlefly smashes its way into the clinic and kidnaps her. He can't let her kill his child, as it may become the only part left of him.

Armed with a shotgun, Borans creeps into the lab but is attacked by Brundlefly, who vomits corrosive bile which eats through his hand and foot. When Veronica begs for his life, he relents. He tells her he will fuse with her and the unborn child to help him become more human; "We'll be the ultimate family." Struggling, she pulls parts of him away as the transformation completes and the fly emerges from the human. It throws her into one telepod and climbs into the other. Borans manages to shoot the cables, and the fly frantically tries to smash its way out of the pod. After the teleportation sequence, the computer announces a successful fusion of Brundlefly and telepod. Through the smoke, a tragic figure half fly and half metal parts crawls towards Veronica. She is terrified, but upon reaching her it takes the gunbarrel in a claw and places it to its head. Hysterical, she finally blasts it out of its misery.

Comment: Cronenberg's crowd-pleaser provides the right shocks at the right moments. His most straightforward horror film understandably broke through to become his biggest hit.

Themes: Cause And Effect: A scientific experiment goes badly wrong, especially for the scientist. Where have we heard that one before? Frankenstein Syndrome/The Absent (Or Mad) Scientist: Brundle's adherence to the principles of scientific investigation culminates in the greatest discovery known to man. One drunken, jealous, reckless act sees him risk, and lose, everything. Mind/Body Schism: Yet again the body revolts, leaving the trapped mind to panic about what the process will lead to. The alienness of the insect mindset is too creepy to contemplate. Altered States/Transformation: Brundlefly really taps into the public's 'eeeeeeugh' response. Audiences watched in horror and fascination as Brundle literally sheds his humanness to become an alien, incomprehensible thing. The fly takes over, but ultimately it is Brundle's guiding humanity that places the shotgun to its head. Postmodern/Existential Uncertainty: Although *The Fly* utilises a straightforward horror structure, there is one important plot point left unresolved – Veronica's pregnancy. Will the insect foetus (if that's what it is) gestate more quickly and find a way to be born? (The poor 1989 sequel, directed by Chris Walas, has a chrysalis containing a human baby. It grows quickly and although it looks human, the process is just waiting to be repeated.) Body/Sexual Horror: The protagonist of Kafka's *Metamorphosis* awakes to find he has become a giant cockroach. For Cronenberg, the metamorphosis is the interesting part, offering the opportunity to show Brundle literally falling apart, preserving his useless human parts (ears, fingernails and, yes, that too) in 'Brundle's Museum Of Natural History.' Spewing acid over Borans' hand and foot, splintering a man's arm and the nightmare 'birth' of the maggot-like foetus are the gleeful icing on the cake. ("It was never just gloop; it was always conceptual gloop.") Slaying Sacred Cows: Science (again), relationships (ditto), childbirth (ditto). Secrets: Brundle has kept his reclusive research a secret for too long. Veronica is the attractive incentive to bring it into the open. Bizarre Organisations: Particle Magazine, owned by Monolith Publishing (!), Bartok Science Industries. Microcosm/Macrocosm: Brundle realises the earth-shattering importance of his discovery. Veronica wants to get the scoop in her book, Borans wants to get the scoop in Particle Magazine. Disease/Ageing/Death: Cronenberg: "To me the film is a metaphor for ageing, a compression of any love affair that goes to the end of one of the lovers' lives." Brundle's initial assessment of his transformation is that he has a "bizarre form of cancer," revisiting *Crimes Of The Future*. Faithless: Tampering with natural sciences always ends in tears. Nature has a way of dealing with the heretics.

Style: The Fly is an interior movie, a play for three actors with few locations. Brundle's warehouse lab is a mysterious place, where home comforts are secondary to scientific equipment, and lighting is in cones which fail to illuminate the dark recesses. In contrast, Veronica's apartment is filled with diffuse light, Borans' office is a high-rise window on the world, and the hospital is antiseptic white. Minimalism is Cronenberg's favourite milieu, and it perfectly contains the unfolding horrific tragedy. The telepods are an inspired piece of production design; the postmodern "nightclub cabinets," or "designer phone booths" are actually modelled on the inverted cylinders of Cronenberg's Ducati motorbike.

Trivia: Martin Scorsese said when he met Cronenberg he expected someone who looked like, "a combination of Arthur Bremmer and Dwight Frye as Renfield in *Dracula*, slobbering for juicy flies. The man who showed up at my apartment in New York looked like a gynaecologist from Beverly Hills." Ironic then that Cronenberg should make a cameo as a gynaecologist in the nightmare sequence.

In 1958, aged 15, Cronenberg saw Neumann's original *The Fly*. In the lobby, a Fox publicity card offered $100 to anyone who could prove the events in the film couldn't happen. Cronenberg told an usher that the huge fly's head made no sense - "Where do the extra molecules and atoms come from for that? If they switched heads, the man should only have a little fly's head!" The usher's response? "Fuck off, kid." Cronenberg took great pains to distance the film from being read as an AIDS allegory; in 1986 the world was in the grip of media panic about the disease.

A coda was filmed but discarded – Veronica has a strange dream of a translucent amber chrysalis on a tree branch, from which hatches a beautiful, butterfly-winged human baby. Another deleted sequence involved teleporting a baboon and a cat together into the third telepod. A horrifying chimeric cat-monkey shrieks out at Brundlefly and skitters across the room before he beats it to death with a pipe - now *that* I would like to have seen! Cronenberg named his protagonist after racing driver Martin Brundle. Borans' first name came from *Heavy Metal* magazine film reviewer Lou Stathis, a fan of Cronenberg's work. Third Assistant Director was Patricia Rozema, who forged her own directorial career with her sleeper hit *I've Heard The Mermaids Singing*.

Verdict: The Fly is a glorious telepod fusion of Cronenberg and traditional horror film; the movie equivalent of an obnoxious kid terrorising a little girl with a big ugly insect. Goldblum makes a definitive quirky, oddball scientist and Cronenberg wrings real pathos from Brundle's doomed metamorphosis. 4/5

"Brothers should be close, don't you think?" – Darryl Revok (*Scanners*)

Dead Ringers (1988)

Director David Cronenberg; Screenplay David Cronenberg, Norman Snider; Novel *Twins* Bari Wood & Jack Geasland

Cast: Jeremy Irons (Elliot & Beverly Mantle), Geneviève Bujold (Claire Niveau), Heidi Von Palleske (Cary), Barbara Gordon (Danuta), Shirley Douglas (Laura), Stephen Lack (Anders Wolleck), Nick Nichols (Leo), Lynn Cormack (Arlene), Damir Andrei (Birchall), Miriam Newhouse (Mrs Bookman)

Credits: Production Company Mantle Clinic II Ltd, In Association With Morgan Creek Productions Inc, With The Participation Of Telefilm Canada; Producers David Cronenberg, Marc Boyman; Executive Producers Carol Baum, Sylvio Tabet; Cinematographer Peter Suschitzky; Editor Ronald Sanders; Music Howard Shore; Production Design Carol Spier; Costume Designer Denise Cronenberg; 115 minutes, 35mm colour, 1.85:1

Story: Toronto, 1954: Identical twin boys Elliot and Beverly Mantle discuss sexual differences between humans and underwater creatures, and ask a neighbourhood girl to have sex with them in a bathtub as an experiment. When told to fuck off, they go home to perform intra-ovular surgery on an anatomical model instead.

Cambridge, Massachusetts, 1967: In a university class the twins examine a corpse using gynaecological instruments made for them. Elliot collects an award for their Mantle Retractor, already the industry standard. In their room he says Bev should have been there, to which his brother replies, "I was."

Toronto, 1988: At the Mantle Clinic Bev examines actress Claire Niveau, in town shooting a miniseries. Excited by what he finds, he informs Elliot, who takes a look for himself. The configuration of her uterus is gynaecologically super rare. He says, "I've often thought there should be beauty contests for the inside of bodies."

Impersonating Bev, Elliot dines with Claire, leaving his brother to return the compliment at a function. Afterwards he relates his conquest to Bev, who is to sample her delights the following day. When Bev arrives, she comes on strong. He is out of his depth, unlike Elliot, who later tells him, "If we didn't share women, you'd still be a virgin." In an intense sex session Elliot ties her up with surgical tubing. For once he refuses to spill the details to Bev, who says he hasn't had an experience until they've shared it.

Bev is the worker; at the clinic and on research data which the suave Elliot uses for academic papers, teaching and fund-raising. Elliot 'gives' Claire to Bev and prescribes her pills "to make sex come on like Nagasaki," but Bev is interested in her as a person. When he self-consciously helps her to read for a part, she asks if he never did impressions as a kid. "Only my brother." He immediately realises his mistake. Avoiding her questions about Elliot, he becomes furious when she mocks his girl's name. She accuses him of schizophrenia, and they take pills to calm down.

Claire's friend Laura is curious about which of the "wonderful Mantle boys" she is dating, and the dollar drops. Claire asks Bev to arrange lunch with Elliot, where she confronts them both. Elliot is amused, but when she storms off Bev is very upset. At an awards dinner he drunkenly interrupts Elliot's speech and causes an embarrassing scene. Next day Elliot reveals he's accepted an associate professorship, leaving Bev to look after the clinic workload and cultivate his drug habit.

When Bev meets Claire by chance, they resume their relationship. In bed with Claire, Elliot lies next to him. They are joined at the chest by a ridge of skin and bone. Claire separates them by ripping the join with her teeth. He awakes screaming.

On a lecture trip, Elliot entertains identical twin call-girls in his hotel suite. He asks one to call him Elli; the other Bev. Beverly's hands are unsteady in operations and he gulps cocktails of pills, having Claire call Danuta to cancel appointments.

When Elliot returns, Claire summons him to her trailer. She is leaving to shoot a film and is worried about Bev being alone. Elliot argues that Bev is never alone but she insists he is, even when he's with her. He suggests rekindling their three-way relationship but she can't; he is too different from his brother. After she goes away, Bev sinks further into addiction and depression. He calls her suite, and assumes the worst when

66

her male secretary Birchall answers. He sobs to Elliot that he loves her and she's betrayed him. In their apartment Elliot dances with occasional girlfriend Cary, and invites Bev to take over. All three dance together, but Bev staggers away and collapses. Elliot gives him mouth-to-mouth resuscitation and he is rushed to hospital.

Elliot has to cover up Bev's addiction, and try to get him off the drugs. When Bev resumes his work at the clinic his behaviour is odd, and he injures a patient, Mrs Bookman. Elliot is worried, especially when Bev insists the instruments were fine, but "the woman's body was all wrong." Bev visits metal sculptor Anders Wolleck, and commissions gynaecological instruments to his own bizarre designs, "for working on mutant women." Danuta finds him shooting up in his office, and resigns.

He uses the grotesque instruments in an operation which goes badly wrong. Elliot stands in for him at the disciplinary hearing, but the instruments are seen as evidence of a disturbed mind and their surgical career is over. Cary begs Elliot to cut himself loose from Bev to save his own reputation, but he can't. He recalls the story of Chang and Eng, the first Siamese twins. One died of a stroke; the other of fright when he awoke to find his brother dead. Instead, Elliot gulps pills in order to "synchronise" with Bev.

Claire calls Bev when she gets back. He barely manages to walk to her apartment. Passing Wolleck's workshop/gallery, he sees his instruments on display and steals them. When he reaches Claire he writes a prescription for Seconal. After a week with her he seems more stable, but his brother hasn't called. He decides to go to Elliot, finding him in a drug-addled mess. They quickly establish a heavy drug regimen, celebrating their birthday with cake, pop and pills. Bev finally finds a use for his instruments; to "separate the siamese twins." He gives Elliot a fix before operating in the empty clinic. Waking from a "terrible dream," he calls to his brother. He shaves, puts on a clean shirt and prepares to go out. In the background Elliot lies on the examination couch, chest and torso opened up like the anatomical model they practised on as boys. The final shot is of Elliot propped against the wall, with Bev lying across his legs, reunited in death.

Comment: At a preview, a doctor asked Cronenberg why he felt so fucking sad afterwards. Cronenberg was surprised. "I can't articulate it... It has to do with this ineffable sadness that is an element of human existence... But the sadness wasn't in the script." I can't believe that's true, because it is in every frame of the finished film. The endings of *Video-*

drome and *The Fly* are rehearsals for the heart-in-fist melancholy of *Dead Ringers*.

Themes: Cause And Effect: The twins' curiosity is shown from their boyhood. Their early experiments fuel their fascination with female biology. Elliot's 'matures' into sexual confidence, while Bev's remains that of a bemused schoolboy. Frankenstein Syndrome/The Absent (Or Mad) Scientist: Two Mad Scientists for the price of one. Mind/Body Schism: Two bodies, one mind? Or a psychic interdependence that has become too powerful? Either way, something has to give. Altered States/Transformation: The twins are Different from the outset, but through their medical genius seem to successfully integrate into the 'normal' world. It can't last. Altering themselves still further by the use of drugs, they come to abhor their biological anomaly, as if they were Siamese twins; their 'separation' is inevitable. Postmodern/Existential Uncertainty: Again Cronenberg attempts to align the viewer's mindset with that of the Outsider(s); to actively experience their Difference rather than watch superficially from a comfortable distance. By killing his brother, Bev has killed himself too. Like Chang and Eng, they can only exist alongside each other. Body/Sexual Horror: The dream sequence makes physical the mental horror of their union; the sexually voracious woman who comes between them symbolically tears at their flesh-bridge with her teeth. Once the join is severed, things cannot be the same. Beverly, the 'wife' of the partnership (even signposted by his female name) finally assumes the dominant role. Like *Videodrome*, *Crash*, *Shivers*, *The Fly* and *M. Butterfly*, the gateway to the mental abyss is opened by female 'contamination' and/or sexual adventure. Slaying Sacred Cows: Families. Relationships. Love. Gynaecologists(!) Secrets: The cornerstone of Elliot and Beverly's relationship, that they keep nothing from each other, changes when Claire enters their lives. Bizarre Organisations: The Mantle Clinic. Microcosm/Macrocosm: The real-life Marcus twins' personal hell became an international news event. As he often does, Cronenberg slips away before that point. Disease/Ageing/Death: Mental illness and drug abuse leads to death just as surely as disease and ageing. Faithless: The twins' unswerving belief in scientific research is undone by their own mental collapse. Their professional access to drugs assists their downfall. The physicians cannot heal themselves, and there is no one else to turn to. The twins' 'soul' cannot sustain two bodies, but is too much for one.

Style: An underrated special effects film. Advanced motion control techniques allowing tracking moves, pans, tilts and focus pulls, plus diffused and moving split-screen work, mattes, acting doubles and on-set video playback seamlessly combine to create the illusion that one person is two, better than ever before. Irons' subtle and convincing performance believably teases out the swaggering Elliot and the timid Beverly. The mise en scène takes you uncomfortably inside their interior environment. If Ronald Mlodzik was the correct fish for Cronenberg's aquarium in the featurettes, then the blue hues of the Mantles' apartment place them inside an updated fishtank for our perusal. The penultimate scene, where Bev goes outside and walks around the postmodern square, looks straight out of *Crimes Of The Future*.

Trivia: Cronenberg dabbled with sculpture during his year in France, making one called *Surgical Instrument For Operating On Mutants*. Seventeen years later, the idea resurfaced in *Dead Ringers*. Cronenberg dropped the scene in the book where the twins have sex. "To me that just felt wrong. If one of them is gay and one of them is not, then already they are different in a very essential way when the point of the whole story should be how similar they are." Another dream sequence was filmed but not used; Bev is horrified by a parasitic twin whose shrunken upper body protrudes from his chest. Cronenberg felt it was too far removed from the rest of the narrative.

Verdict: Dead Ringers is super-competent. Like *The Fly*, essentially a play for three actors (but by the magic of film, two), its airless claustrophobia and existential angst are masterfully executed. Only David Cronenberg could have made this film. That it is such a depressing experience should not blind one to its excellence. 4/5

"Their purpose is entirely opaque to me, like the purposes of so many others" – Adrian Tripod (*Crimes Of The Future*)

Naked Lunch (!991)

Director/Screenplay David Cronenberg; Novel *The Naked Lunch* William S Burroughs

Cast: Peter Weller (Bill Lee), Judy Davis (Joan Frost/Joan Lee), Ian Holm (Tom Frost), Julian Sands (Yves Cloquet), Roy Scheider (Doctor Benway), Monique Mercure (Fadela), Nicholas Campbell (Hank), Michael Zelniker (Martin), Robert A Silverman (Hans), Joseph Scorsiani (Kiki), Yuval Daniel (Hafid), John Friesen (Hauser), Sean McCann (O'Brien), Howard Jerome (AJ Cohen)

Credits: Producer Jeremy Thomas; Co-producer Gabriella Martinelli; Cinematographer Peter Suschitzky; Editor Ronald Sanders; Music Howard Shore; Sound Bryan Day; Production Designer Carol Spier; Creature Creation & Design Chris Walas Inc; Special Effects Supervisor Jim Isaac; Costume Designer Denise Cronenberg; 115 minutes, 35mm colour, 1.85:1

Story: New York City, 1953: While spraying an apartment, Bill Lee runs out of bug powder, to the annoyance of his employer AJ Cohen, who rations it carefully. In a bar, two writer friends debate technique. Martin endlessly rewrites; Hank disagrees with any form of self-censorship. Bill's opinion is "Exterminate all rational thought." He no longer writes, because it's "too dangerous." Bill arrives home to find his wife Joan shooting up the powder. She tells him he should try it too: "It's a Kafka high – you feel like a bug."

Bill is arrested for possession, and at the station narcs Hauser and O'Brien leave him in a room with a giant beetle. Gorging itself on the powder, it asks him to rub it into its sphincter-like 'lips' on its back, and says it's his "case officer." His assignment is to kill his wife, who is an inhuman agent for Interzone Incorporated. He crushes it with his shoe and escapes. He tells Joan he's been busted for bug powder and he's hallucinating. A work colleague gives him a card for a Dr Benway, who can cure his addiction. The mysterious Benway dispenses black centipede powder, which he says is like "an agent who's come to believe his own cover story but who's in there, in a larval state, just waiting for the proper moment to hatch out." Passing a market stall selling giant centipedes, Bill feels nauseous. When he gets home, Hank is fucking Joan while Martin recites stream of consciousness prose. He injects himself and Joan, then says "I guess it's about time for our William Tell routine." She places a glass on her head and he shoots, killing her.

In a bar a young eastern-looking man introduces him to a mugwump, a bizarre gangly alien creature who recommends a Clark-Nova portable typewriter for his report on his wife's death, to be written in Interzone. It hands him a ticket. In a pawnshop, he exchanges his gun for a Clark-Nova.

In Interzone, a North African coastal enclave, he and many other men type reports. He is propositioned by German bon vivant Hans, whose drug factory synthesises black centipede 'meat.' In Bill's room, his drug haze is interrupted by his Clark-Nova's semi-transformation into a beetle - a bugwriter - which tells him that homosexuality is an agent's best cover. At a party he meets expat American writers Tom and Joan Frost. Joan looks like Bill's dead wife. Tom confesses to Bill that he is killing her slowly, using their housekeeper Fadela. He does this telepathically – his lips say something else entirely. Bill crashes out on Interzone beach, and in the morning is picked up by enigmatic Swiss dandy Cloquet. The Frosts tell him he impressed Cloquet, and Tom lends him his sleek Martinelli typewriter. Bill writes that he seems addicted to something that doesn't really exist. He awakes to find his bugwriter devouring the Martinelli, which it indignantly informs him is an enemy agent. It suggests he seduce Joan Frost for information.

He goes to see Joan and confesses to wrecking Tom's Martinelli. She says he has another, in Arabic - a Mujahedin (!) As she types something erotic, it mutates into organic form. A vaginal orifice opens, into which she thrusts her fingers as Bill caresses her. Their arousal escalates; the typewriter transforms into a 'sex blob,' and jumps on them in uncontrolled ecstasy. They are interrupted by housekeeper/witch Fadela, who whips the thing over the balcony. It crashes to the street in front of an incensed Tom, a typewriter once more. Bill and Joan walk through the casbah, finding Fadela with her coven on a stall selling black centipede meat. Joan is in her power.

The bugwriter tells Bill he was programmed to kill his wife. She was a "special case," an elite-corps centipede. Tom storms in for his Martinelli, only to find it smashed, and captures the bugwriter in exchange. On Interzone beach, Bill is found by Hank and Martin, who encourage him to complete his book *Naked Lunch*, which they have been receiving in instalments. He doesn't know what they're talking about. They get on the bus back.

Bill passes out in an alley and is helped by Kiki, who takes the broken Martinelli to a forge where a new mugwump-head typewriter is cast. The 'mugwriter' tells Bill that Benway is behind Interzone Inc. His power is based on the black centipede meat; however, he's too elusive to catch. Bill and Kiki take a ride in Cloquet's "wonderful car," and Bill relates a story about a man who taught his asshole to talk, but found it aspired to a life of its own. At his sumptuous house, Cloquet takes Kiki into the bedroom. When Bill investigates, Cloquet has become a giant centipede, literally sucking Kiki dry inside a huge cage. Bill takes the mugwriter to Frost to swap for his Clark-Nova. It has been tortured, but before expiring it tells Bill to go to Hans' drug factory in the medina, where he'll find Interzone Inc.

The factory is now a dispensary, where mugwumps are strung up and highly addictive jissom is milked from teat-like protrusions on their heads. Fadela supervises the process, while Hans and other dissipated addicts consume the jissom. Fadela reveals herself to be Benway in a prosthetic disguise. Bill agrees to work for Benway in Annexia, as long as Joan can accompany him.

Bill drives a strange red half-track vehicle to the border, where the guards demand proof that he is a writer. Bill wakes Joan and says it's time for the William Tell routine. She places a glass on her head, and once again he shoots her. He is devastated, but the guards merely welcome him to Annexia and wave him on.

Comment: Cronenburroughs is, perhaps unsurprisingly, more Cronenberg than Burroughs. After all, Brundlefly is more fly than Brundle. "The film has to be something that still deserves to be called *Naked Lunch*, accurately reflecting some of the tone of Burroughs, what his life stands for, and what his work has been – a combination of Burroughsian material but put into a structure that's not very Burroughsian." But very Cronenbergian.

Themes: Cause And Effect: Go figure - as long as you're on junk. Frankenstein Syndrome/The Absent (Or Mad) Scientist: Every man is his own Mad Scientist. Benway may run Interzone Inc, but he is an invention of Bill/Lee Burroughs. Writers and Mad Scientists have their own special relationship. Mind/Body Schism: In the grip of The Sickness (junk abuse), the mind has little idea what it, or the body, is doing. Lee, like Burroughs, has no recollection of writing the 'novel' he sends his friends. Altered States/Transformation: Like *Videodrome*, the narrative is an altered state. Interzone is an escapist fantasy. Drugs allow you to enter, but the only 'escape' is further into their trap. Postmodern/Existential Uncertainty: Modernism changed emphasis from what is perceived to the act of perception. Postmodernism questioned the validity of perception itself. To post-postmodernists like Cronenberg and Burroughs, subjectivity is under constant attack. Perception and identity are mutable concepts. Metaphor, symbol and stream of consciousness are foregrounded. Burroughs said language itself is a virus from outer space. The act of creation is dangerous to the creator; the abyss awaits in various guises. Body/Sexual Horror: Homosexuality may be an agent's best cover, but Cronenberg counters Burroughs' predatory gay sensibility with his own heterosexuality (Cloquet becomes half-insect to consume his victims; Bill Lee refuses homosexual assignments). Alien lounge-lizards like the Mugwumps present a different sexuality still. Their drug (jissom) is milked from penis/teat extremities on their heads (sex as addiction). Benway's disguise is a female prosthesis. Bill's literary muse is a woman, the same woman, whom he is doomed to 'kill,' i.e. betray, over and over. Slaying Sacred Cows: Where does one start? Secrets: 'Normal' life. How can people do the same job for years, raise kids, chat to neighbours over the garden fence? Bizarre Organisations: Interzone Incorporated. Microcosm/Macrocosm: The act of creation is the microcosm, its distribution to an audience is the macrocosm. Disease/Ageing/

Death: The real disease is the human propensity to addiction and self-abuse that tears life apart, but makes for interesting observation. Faithless: Burroughs' Sickness was as far away from faith as it gets – junkie, queer, murderer. Legs McNeil wrote, "More than any other man, Burroughs is responsible for introducing deviancy into the mainstream of American culture." Again, Cronenberg's individual constructs his own reality, outside (and regardless of) social and religious norms.

Style: The 50s look is pervasive, reinforced by chiaroscuro lighting and warm, almost soft-focus tones. Brown is the predominant colour, blues provide moments of 'clarity.' The film's ambience has to reinforce the hallucinatory, albeit consistent, vision of Bill Lee, who never leaves New York, but escapes into his own fantasy of writing. Peter Suschitzky wanted an expressionistic, Kafka look. "I suggested that we do the sets like *Dr Caligari*, but David said 'There's enough craziness in the film as it is...'" Carol Spier concurs, "With David you can only go so far with stylizing. He likes his settings pretty normal because all the other things... are so abnormal."

Trivia: Although Interzone is a subconscious state, it was also Tangiers' International Zone, where Burroughs wrote the book. Artists flocked there to create (or not) in a tax-free and liberal environment. Synchronicity saw *Naked Lunch* emerge as one of a series of films about writers/writing around the same time, including Steven Soderbergh's *Kafka*, Joel and Ethan Coen's superb *Barton Fink* and Phil Kaufman's *Henry And June*. PhilDickian paranoia is again present. In *A Scanner Darkly*'s hallucinatory journey through addiction, narc cop Fred poses as dealer Bob Arctor, to investigate a brain-toxic drug called 'Substance D' (death). In his drug fugue he literally forgets his own identity and informs on himself, ending up a human husk.

Verdict: Cronenberg's brave attempt to synthesise Burroughs deserves points for integrity and invention, but paradoxically, the perfect director for the project becomes the reason it ultimately fails to catch alight. For me, *Naked Lunch* calls for bravura stylisation; a cinematic tour de force pulling out all the stops, attacking the subject matter with an arsenal. Even *Trainspotting* memorably flayed open the thorny topic of addiction. Cronenberg's introverted, relaxed, by now predictable methods don't have the razor-edge energy to cut you like the novel. Instead of Interzone, we have comfort-zone. As a Cronenberg film, this punches its weight. As *Naked Lunch*, it's in trouble on the ropes. 3/5

"30 seconds after you're born you have a past. And 60 seconds after that you start to lie to yourself about it." – Juliana Kelly (*The Brood*)

M. Butterfly (1993)

Director David Cronenberg; Screenplay David Henry Hwang (Based On His Play)

Cast: Jeremy Irons (René Gallimard), John Lone (Song Liling), Barbara Sukowa (Jeanne Gallimard), Ian Richardson (Ambassador Toulon), Annabel Leventon (Frau Bauden), Shizuko Hoshi (Comrade Chin), Vernon Dobtcheff (Agent Etancelin)

Credits: Production Company Geffen Pictures In Association With M. Butterfly Productions Inc; Producer Gabriella Martinelli; Executive Producers David Henry Hwang, Philip Sandhaus; Cinematographer Peter Suschitzky; Editor Ronald Sanders; Music Howard Shore; Sound Bryan Day; Production Designer Carol Spier; Costume Designer Denise Cronenberg; 102 minutes, 35mm colour, 1.85:1

Story: Beijing, 1964. Mild-mannered René Gallimard, an accountant at the French embassy, watches captivated as Opera diva Song Liling sings a selection from *Madame Butterfly*. Afterwards he says she has opened his eyes to the beauty in the tragic tale, but she pours scorn on his romanticised western ideal of the submissive oriental woman. He tells his wife the Chinese can't stand *Madame Butterfly* because "the white man gets the girl."

Three weeks later René musters the courage to visit the Opera again. Although he and Song only talk, he lies to his wife about his whereabouts. Song next entertains him in her parlour, a potentially scandalous action in a country "rooted 2000 years in the past." When he kisses her, she asks him to leave. At Frau Bauden's party he is accosted by angry embassy employees whose expenses he has refused. Song writes him letters which he doesn't answer.

Ambassador Toulon notes his personality change ("You've become this new, aggressive, overconfident thing"), and appoints René Vice-Consul, in charge of setting up a new intelligence-gathering operation. He rushes to Song, and demands to know if she's his butterfly. She shyly admits she is, although to protect her modesty she insists on remaining clothed as they make love, watched by the prying eyes of her maid. Their courtship continues with a trip to the Great Wall.

The ambassador asks Gallimard's opinion on Vietnam for a report. He says the Americans must show strength, as the Oriental will always bow to a superior force. Song feeds him such misinformation, and relays his comments on American troop movements to local Party official Comrade Chin, who is disgusted to find American movie-star magazines in her parlour. She counters "I'm trying my best to become somebody else." At another of Frau Bauden's parties, Gallimard embarks on an "extra extra-marital affair" with her. On his next visit to Song, he demands to see her naked. She tells him she is pregnant and must go to her parents' village, as is the custom, from which she will bring him back a son. He is delighted. She goes to Chin and requests a male Chinese baby with blond hair.

Passing a Red Guard demonstration, Gallimard witnesses the burning of opera costumes. The ambassador advises caution, as they have become a powerful movement. Song visits Gallimard with their 'son.' He proposes marriage, but she is marched away by Red Guard militia who have declared all artists criminals under the Cultural Revolution. Gallimard is sent home for wrongly analysing the Chinese and Vietnamese political situations. On a last visit, he finds Song's courtyard quarters full of peasants. Meanwhile Song sweats in a re-education camp, as a loudspeaker voice declares hard labour will transform them into citizens of the future under the tutelage of Chairman Mao.

Paris, 1968. Watching a performance of *Madame Butterfly*, Gallimard's eyes fill with tears. Outside, pro-Communist students riot and attack the police. His apartment décor is austere Chinese chic. One day Song reappears, and he is overjoyed. He works as a motorcycle courier, carrying diplomatic pouches. He is soon arrested by Etancelin, a government agent.

At his trial for espionage, he is confronted by the crushing spectacle of Song in a suit and tie, unmistakably a man. Much to the court's incredulity, Song tells how Gallimard gave him access to the diplomatic pouches to protect their son back in China. When asked if he thinks Gallimard knew he was a man, he speaks of his oriental ways of love, "out of which I invented myself, just for him." In a police van en route to jail, Song finally disrobes, bitterly reminding Gallimard he's still the same person. Gallimard rejects his advances, destroyed by the revelation of Song's true self when what he loved was the lie.

In prison, Gallimard gives a one-man performance, admitting his story has given the whole of France a good laugh. As Song boards a plane to China, having been extradited, Gallimard plays a tape of *Madame Butterfly* and relates the tale as if he himself were the tragic oriental woman who loved an unworthy man. In oriental clothes, heavy Chinese make-up and wig, he says he has found the perfect sacrificial woman, far from China. In front of all the inmates and warders, he kneels forward and slits his throat.

Comment: It is amazing how Cronenberg assimilates other writers' material into his own consistent world-view. "René is creating a reality for himself... He is creating the opera of his life, preparing to become the diva of it... Song is helping him. I find that a very interesting version of stuff that I've done before but probably would not have done that way."

Themes: Cause And Effect: Like Max Renn, Gallimard's preconceptions and naïveté draw him into a web of intrigue and self-deception from which he cannot escape. Frankenstein Syndrome/The Absent (Or Mad) Scientist: Gallimard constructs his own fantasy creature, based on his romanticised cultural ideals and sexual desires, blinded to the 'reality' of the situation. Frankenstein falls in love with his monster. Mind/Body Schism: Gallimard's desire is so strong that his body seems able to convince his mind that Song is a woman, or represses the knowledge so that his sexuality can function without revulsion. Altered States/Transformation: Song transforms himself (herself?) into Gallimard's ideal Oriental woman by inventing a fake ancient Chinese sexuality, to maintain a precarious social position and obtain political information. Gallimard transforms himself in turn, to allow himself to fall for the deception. Cronenberg's protagonists often transform or reinvent themselves through dissatisfaction with their lives, or their reality. In addition, a cultural transformation is played out against the volatile Chinese political situation and the symbolic narrative of *Madame Butterfly*. Postmodern/Existential Uncertainty: No fixed concepts; body, mind, sexuality, identity, culture and status are all subjective and in constant flux. Body/Sexual Horror: Gallimard's expression when confronted in court by Song's true sex is a stunning moment. "Only a man knows how a woman is supposed to act." If Gallimard was certain Song was a woman, it may never have occurred to him that a man may be able to convincingly mimic their actions. Just as Beverly Mantle reversed his 'female' role in the twins' relationship, Gallimard's role changes from dominant western male to the doomed female role of deceived lover. ("Jeremy's a combination of Beverly and Elliot in this movie. He's Beverly aspiring more to be Elliot. We joked about it.") Song is 'forced' to be homosexual, but really wants to do it anyway. It may not be a true identity, but it's the best he has. Slaying Sacred Cows: Male/female relationships (as ever), cultural interaction, official status. The French diplomatic service is portrayed as clueless to the Chinese mindset, bureaucratic and complacent. Secrets: The biggest secret of all is Song's gender. State secrets are the currency of his/her 'love.' Bizarre Organisations: The Red Guard! Microcosm/Macrocosm: Again, a personal situation becomes a national/

international issue. The bizarre real-life scenario was widely reported. Disease/Ageing/Death: Gallimard dies from a very common disease – love. Faithless: The only faith Gallimard has is in Song; when it is shattered he commits ritual suicide.

Style: Following the interiorised narratives of *The Fly, Dead Ringers* and *Naked Lunch*, Cronenberg opens *M. Butterfly* out, with many location exteriors in China and France, actually including a vista of the Great Wall! Even in this setting, the framing strongly foregrounds the two human figures, symbolically positioned next to a huge drop. Despite the exteriors, Cronenberg's interiors are as important as ever. Chinese iconography is alien, emphasising 2000 years of difference. The mysterious dark recesses of Song's quarters contrast with the light airiness of the embassy. The key scene where Gallimard is forced to confront that which he'd desired for so long, Song's nakedness, takes place in the bare confines of a police van. ("That's the scene that most people put down as favourite. Thank God it worked, and again it's two people in a fucking room.")

Trivia: Cronenberg felt the film's impact was undermined by the surprise popularity of Neil Jordan's *The Crying Game*. The revelation that Stephen Rea's character assuages his guilt over the death of a black British soldier by taking care of, and then falling in love with his girlfriend, who turns out to be a man, hit him hard. He grafted on a prologue explaining in advance that Song was a man, but this produced unease about the sex scenes and was dropped.

One major problem is the shallow Western attitude to sex. Many people just didn't buy that Gallimard could have sex with Song without knowing she was a man. Cronenberg was candid in his frustration that people believed "...naturally he would have wanted to stick his cock up her cunt. Only that satisfies a real guy, so how come he didn't? ...I think people have got to accept how weird people really are. In the Victorian era men certainly went 20 years without ever seeing their wife's cunt. It's not so amazing." The real Gallimard, Bernard Boursicot, and his paramour Shi Pei Pu, had sexual relations for that length of time.

Verdict: For a drama about a diplomat in a foreign country, played out against the backdrop of the Chinese Cultural Revolution, *M. Butterfly* is surprisingly intimate, although let's face it, Cronenberg is never going to make a David Lean movie. It's an interesting film, though hardly radical; maybe even charming. It fits the Cronenberg Project like a glove, but the glove was perhaps becoming too comfortable (hence *Crash*?) Good as always but well within limits. 3/5

8. Man-Machine II: Road Rape

"Is it life, or is it Memorex?" – Seth Brundle (*The Fly*)

Crash (1996)

Director/Screenplay/Producer David Cronenberg; Novel JG Ballard

Cast: James Spader (James Ballard), Holly Hunter (Dr Helen Remington), Elias Koteas (Robert Vaughan), Deborah Kara Unger (Catherine Ballard), Rosanna Arquette (Gabrielle), Peter MacNeill (Colin Seagrave), Cheryl Swarts (Vera Seagrave), John Stonehouse Jr (Brett Trask)

Credits: Production Company Alliance Communications Corporation; Executive Producers Robert Lantos, Jeremy Thomas; Co-Executive Producers Andras Hamori, Chris Auty; Co-Producers Stephane Reichel, Marilyn Stonehouse; Music Howard Shore; Cinematographer Peter Suschitzky; Editor Ronald Sanders; Production Designer Carol Spier; Costume Designer Denise Cronenberg; Trainee Assistant Director Cassandra Cronenberg (David's daughter); 96 minutes, 35mm colour, 1.85:1

Story: In an aircraft hangar, against a gleaming plane, Catherine Ballard is taken from behind by a swarthy guy. In a filmset camera room, producer James Ballard takes a camera girl over a table. In the Ballards' high-rise apartment, they calmly discuss their respective trysts. When told he didn't come, she distantly replies, "Poor darling. Maybe the next one, maybe the next one..." Ballard takes her from behind as she leans over the balcony, set against tiny freeway traffic below.

Later, as Ballard drives and riffles through papers, he loses control. The car jumps carriageways and smashes into another head-on. The driver plunges through Ballard's windshield; his hand bears the imprint of the bonnet insignia. The female passenger fumbles with her seat belt, exposing her breast. She and Ballard stare at each other in shock.

Ballard shuffles along a hospital corridor, leg encased in steel pins and scaffolding. The passenger, Dr Helen Remington, gives him a withering look as she walks stiffly by. A man in white overalls, holding photographs of crash wounds, examines his injuries with great interest. In his isolated ward, Ballard and Catherine indulge in a spot of mutual masturbation as she describes the shattered wreck of his car. After going home, he scans traffic through binoculars. He says there seems to be more traffic since the accident. Getting behind the wheel again, he drives to examine his car at the pound. Helen Remington is also there. He takes her to the airport, where she works in immigration, and almost has another accident when a car cuts in front. She suggests the airport garage, where they fuck frenetically. At home, sex with Catherine is more urgent.

Helen takes Ballard to an 'event' staged by the enigmatic Vaughan: a reconstruction of James Dean's fatal 1955 crash in his racing Porsche,

'Little Bastard.' Ballard recognises Vaughan as the man from the hospital. The accident is restaged without safety gear for Vaughan or his two stunt drivers, Seagrave and Trask. Watched by the small crowd, the two cars impact at speed. Trask is OK. Vaughan struggles painfully from the wrecked Porsche, but Seagrave is only semi-conscious. Over the PA Vaughan announces, "James Dean died of a broken neck and became immortal," as police sirens sound, scattering the crowd into the woods. They reach Vaughan's battered black Lincoln convertible. As he drives, he fingers Helen as Ballard watches curiously. At an unkempt communal house, Vera Seagrave attends to her husband while callipered crash victim Gabrielle offers joints. Everyone is wasted. Vaughan talks to the concussed Seagrave about recreating Jayne Mansfield's fatal crash. Producing an album of crash photographs, he describes his project as "the reshaping of the human body by modern technology."

Ballard and Catherine drive in separate cars. At an intersection, Vaughan draws up behind Catherine's silver sports car and follows aggressively before she pulls off the road. When Ballard takes her from the rear once more, she incorporates Vaughan into the act, asking if Ballard would like to sodomise him in his big car. In the airport garage, Helen and Ballard fuck. Discussing her sexual exploits in cars, she admits to a fantasy of Vaughan photographing them as if they were traffic accidents. Later at the house, the group smoke joints and watch crash-test videos.

Driving around airport perimeter roads, Ballard connects the 1963 Lincoln with JFK's assassination. Vaughan tells him "the car crash is a fertilising rather than a destructive event – a liberation of sexual energy... of those who have died, with an intensity that is impossible in any other form." It is clear that this is Vaughan's real desire – the ultimate existential experience. He picks up an airport hooker and fucks her while Ballard drives and watches in the mirror.

As Catherine and Ballard leave the studio, Vaughan is questioned by the police about the death of a pedestrian near the airport. He is shaken, and Ballard drives his car. On the freeway they encounter a multi-vehicle accident. Vaughan takes crash photographs, then stages more using Catherine as a model. The emergency services are too busy to care. In the front wreck, Vaughan finds the dead Seagrave, dressed as Jayne Mansfield, complete with scalped wig and dead dog in the back. He is amazed that Seagrave went through with it on his own. After Ballard finds blood on Vaughan's car, they go through a car wash. In the back

79

seat, Vaughan brutally fucks Catherine under the gaze of an entranced Ballard, who later examines her bruises in silence.

In a showroom, Gabrielle is helped into a Mercedes by an embarrassed salesman as Ballard looks on, amused. At the airport garage, Ballard arranges her broken body in order to access a healed crash-wound in her rear thigh. Vaughan phones Ballard to witness his "prophetic" medical tattoo; a steering-column indentation on his torso. He encourages Ballard to have a small insignia on his thigh. Later, in a junkyard, Ballard and Vaughan finally have sex. Afterwards, as Ballard sits behind the wheel of a wrecked car, Vaughan slams into it. Next day, Catherine's car has also been rammed.

Ballard drives around the airport perimeter. Vaughan's car launches out of nowhere; he is in a delirium as he toys with the sports car, ramming it playfully before swerving over a parapet and landing on a coach below. Ballard surveys the carnage.

In the pound, Gabrielle and Helen make love in the wreck of the Lincoln. Ballard goes to reclaim it. On the open road, he drives it as recklessly as Vaughan, overtaking insanely in pursuit of Catherine. He rams her car, running it off the road and down an embankment. He stumbles painfully down to her. She has been thrown clear, skirt around her waist. He caresses her, and when she says she's alright, he takes her from behind, saying "Maybe the next one..."

Comment: Ballard said of the film "...the surrealists discovered if you're going to present extraordinary subject matter, put your characters into dinner jackets." The Dadaists knew that for their anti-art movement to succeed, they paradoxically had to create art. Cronenberg remakes Ballard in his own image and tears down the façade of cinema and external world in his quiet, unassuming manner, by integrating the novel into his quest "to show the unshowable, to speak the unspeakable."

Themes: Cause And Effect: Not this time. There is no 'normal' world; the characters are already damaged beyond repair. Frankenstein Syndrome/The Absent (Or Mad) Scientist: Aleister Crowley as pseudo-scientist; Vaughan's 'Project' is part of the real Mad Scientist's plan (Cronenberg's). Helen says of him "he was a specialist in computerised international traffic systems. I don't know what he is now." (Read: Christ knows what he is now.) Uniquely, Vaughan's Project *intentionally* culminates in his own death. Mind/Body Schism: The characters are creatures of abstract(ed) thought who synthesise their curious bodily urges with those of others. Again the mind's desire places the body in danger. Altered States/Transformation: The car crash is the catalyst for alteration; of mindset, sexuality, purpose and body. Postmodern/Existential Uncertainty: Like *Videodrome*, a White Paper on existentialism. The orgasm is possibly the epitome of existential angst – climax as anti-climax. Should the earth move? ("Maybe the next one, darling. Maybe the next one...") But of course, it never does. Is sex humanity's most meaningless activity? If anyone can do it, where's its intellectual merit? *Crash* is a cool, collected response to the Jerry Springer generation. Body/Sexual Horror: Crash injuries, mangled bodies, real-time crashes without Hollywood slo-mo or multiple angles, sex with wounds. The close-up of Vaughan's viscid fingers on the leather upholstery after brutally fingerfucking Catherine is more *Alien* than *Basic Instinct*. Slaying Sacred Cows: Modern life is stale and tedious. Sex is unsatisfactory. People are shallow zombies who cannot know themselves, much less each other. It's party time again. Secrets: Life, the universe and everything. Bizarre Organisations: A bizarre disorganisation. Vaughan's crew are the motliest bunch of droogs since Frank Booth's in *Blue Velvet*. Microcosm/Macrocosm: Vaughan's final gesture is as futile as Max Renn's. Immortality of the James Dean or Jayne Mansfield kind is not open to mere mortals. Disease/Ageing/Death: In Godard's *A Bout De Souffle* (*Breathless*), novelist Parvulesco says his greatest wish is to achieve immortality, then die. Vaughan's is to achieve the eternal orgasm but, like Max, his suicide is the fool's solution. Faithless: Philip K Dick concluded that if God exists, and Man is made in God's image, then God is seriously flawed, maybe even insane. Cronenberg's 'children' exist in a spiritual vacuum that is the antithesis of Dick's soul-searching. For them, God is an irrelevance.

Style: The film's formal system is Cronenberg's most impressive, integrated and downright European since *Videodrome*; Kieslowski out of Antonioni. Iain Sinclair writes "The low-key performances, the subdued light, the lacklustre physical permutations, all contribute to an overwhelming sense of alienation." Passages like "Light like the interior skyscape of a patient awaiting brain surgery," and "The actors aren't delivering a script, they're under hypnosis" perfectly capture the air of postmodern ennui. The characters are plastic automata, programmed to observe but not connect, to sexualise but not eroticise, to inhabit but not engage. The bare-metal performances, locations and décor are astonishing. Car bodies dominate human ones; cutting across the frame, body parts isolated in abstract close-ups. The assimilation of Ballard's semiological lattice-work of signs and numbers is a triumphant paradox; chaos held in stasis. Alienation is not a state of mind, but a statement of fact.

Sex scenes become plot and character development. Sex from behind, facing the camera, disconnected from each other; from everything. Sex in aircraft hangars, multi-storey carparks, cramped car interiors, underpasses, slip roads, embankments, car wash, hospital; familiar locations devoid of familiarity, stripped of comfort. Steely-blue lighting, warm but vacant flesh tones, black-ant traffic on bleached freeways, rain-flecked, despairing dark night drives. In the absence of Meaning, fetishising the car's capacity to redefine the human body is a kind of ACME Instant Metaphysical Catharsis kit. The amazing thing is, it works.

Trivia: Ballard playfully suggested Cronenberg could have named the protagonist after himself, as Ballard had done in the novel. At the 1996 Cannes Film Festival, Holly Hunter took grave exception to a journalist's line of questioning, abusing him to the point of physical threat. An Indonesian festival lost international credibility by removing Rosanna Arquette's character because she wears leg-braces and callipers ("Physical disabilities are totally taboo there, so *sex* with someone disabled...") Even Cronenberg's agent implored him not to do the movie, telling him it would end his career. He subsequently changed agents. Vaughan's ultimate goal in the novel was understandably dropped - to smash into Elizabeth Taylor's Rolls-Royce!

Verdict: Of all Cronenberg's films, *Crash* is the hardest to judge using normal criteria. It just won't work. *Crash* is unique; its whole is like nothing else and its parts are only like Cronenberg films. It's unsurprising that many people loathe it because of its absolute challenge to what a movie should be. Cronenberg demonstrates he has not lost his ability or desire to make razor-edged, antagonistic cinema, and that he is still the person best equipped to do so. For me, his best film since *Videodrome*, no question. 4.5/5

9. Mind Games II

"After all, there's nothing real outside our perception of reality, is there?"
– Brian O'Blivion (*Videodrome*)

eXistenZ (1999)

Director/Screenplay David Cronenberg
Cast: Jennifer Jason Leigh (Allegra Geller), Jude Law (Ted Pikul), Willem Dafoe (Gas), Ian Holm (Kiri Vinokur), Don McKellar (Yevgeny Nourish), Callum Keith Rennie (Hugo Carlaw), Sarah Polley (Merle), Christopher Eccleston (Levi), Robert A Silverman (D'Arcy Nader), Oscar Hsu (Chinese Waiter), Kris Lemche (Noel Dichter)

Credits: Production Company Alliance Atlantis And Serendipity Point Films In Association With Natural Nylon, With The Participation Of Telefilm Canada; Producers Robert Lantos, Andras Hamori, David Cronenberg; Associate Producer Sandra Tucker; Co-Producers Michael MacDonald, Damon Bryant, Bradley Adams; Cinematographer Peter Suschitzky; Editor Ronald Sanders; Music Howard Shore; Production Designer Carol Spier; Visual And Special Effects Supervisor Jim Isaac; Costume Designer Denise Cronenberg; 3rd Assistant Director Cassandra Cronenberg; 93 minutes, 35mm colour, 1.85:1

Story: In a church hall, Antenna Research selects twelve people to test *eXistenZ*, the new game by "game-pod Goddess" Allegra Geller. She takes the stage to rapturous applause. Security man Ted Pikul scans late arrival Dichter for weapons or recording devices. The game begins when Allegra downloads *eXistenZ* from her organic MetaFlesh game pod into the pod of each volunteer, whose nervous systems are connected via 'umbycords.' Dichter produces a gun which looks made of bone, shouting "Death to the demoness Allegra Geller. Death to Antenna Research." He fires, hitting her in the shoulder, and also shoots Antenna's host Levi before he is himself shot. In the stampede, Levi urges Pikul to get Allegra out and trust no one.

Driving along country roads, Allegra is not pleased to find Pikul is unarmed, and is in actuality a "PR nerd." He removes the 'bullet' from her shoulder; a human tooth. They stop at a motel (helpfully labelled 'Motel'). Allegra wants to find out what's going on by entering the game, but Pikul confesses he has never had a bioport fitted. He sarcastically suggests that in the countryside, at midnight, why not just get one at a local country gas station?

At a place helpfully labelled 'Country Gas Station' the attendant 'Gas' is overawed to meet Allegra. He implants an illegal, unregistered bioport into the terrified Pikul's spine while Allegra waits outside, watching a strange two-headed lizard creature. When she jacks Pikul into her pod, it immediately short-circuits. She is furious, as the pod contains the only version of *eXistenZ* and now she can't get in, or get it out. Pikul insists the "neural surge" was not his fault. Gas levels a shotgun at Allegra and admits sabotaging the bioport ("it's all over the countryside - $5 million for her dead body"). Pikul shoots him with the bioport gun.

They drive to a ski lodge in the forest. Pikul is taken aback by the two-headed creature, which Allegra calls a "mutated amphibian." Game expert Kiri Vinokur operates on Allegra's damaged pod, which he tells Pikul is "grown from fertilised amphibian eggs stuffed with synthetic DNA." He also replaces Pikul's bioport. In a secluded chalet, Allegra and Pikul at last jack into the game.

The scene subtly shifts to D'Arcy Nader's Game Emporium. Their clothes and look are different: Pikul is more stylish, while Allegra is sexier. When he asks the rules, she says "You have to play the game to find out why you're playing the game." Nader gives them micro-pods which he says will give them new identities. After a brief romantic interlude, the scene switches again, to...

The Trout Farm. Pikul seems to know how to deftly fillet strange amphibians. Yevgeny Nourish explains it is a factory for making game pods, and recommends the lunchtime special at the Chinese restaurant in the forest. Pikul finds Allegra. Feeling "a little disconnected," he pauses the game for a moment. At the ski chalet, he is concerned that now even real life feels like a game. Back at the restaurant, the special arrives. Pikul assembles a gristle-gun from its innards. He levels it at Allegra, then turns and shoots the Chinese waiter in the face. A dog runs off with the 'gun.' Nourish is delighted they passed the test. Outside, he shows them breeding pools – the restaurant is a cover for developing amphibians as undetectable weapons. Pikul is to resume his work at 'Cortical Systematics' to maintain his cover. They have proven themselves as "true and trustworthy realists."

At the Game Emporium, Nader's assistant Carlaw (a Realist Underground agent) tells them it was a mistake to kill the waiter, who was their contact. Nader is dead and Nourish works for Cortical Systematics. Back at the Trout Farm, Pikul is uneasy about the game's haphazard rules, or absence of them. Allegra is amused ("it's a game everybody's already playing"). She jacks into a diseased game pod, in order to upload the disease and transmit it to other pods. Her system can't handle it. Pikul cuts her umbycord, but it jets blood. Nourish enters with a flame thrower and torches the pod, which ejects a cloud of spores. Allegra plunges the knife into his back, and he sets the place alight. Pikul says it looks as if they lost the game. Suddenly they're back in the chalet. Allegra's pod looks sick, and she realises they have imported the disease from the game. She tells Pikul that Vinokur must have given him an infected bioport.

An explosion blows in the windows. Carlaw appears, as Che Guevara, shouting that the uprising has begun, and blasts her pod. Pikul tells the hysterical Allegra they must still be in the game. In the forest, a mini-war is raging. Carlaw aims the gun at Allegra, but is shot by Vinokur, who tells her *eXistenZ* was copied into another pod and will be fine as long as she pledges her allegiance to Cortical Systematics. She shoots him with Carlaw's gun. Pikul snatches it from her, saying if this *is* the real world then she just killed someone. He finally reveals himself as an assassin, but she had guessed in the restaurant. She detonates a charge in his bioport, blowing out his spine.

Allegra comes to in the church hall with the others. Pikul is now a player, as are Gas, Dichter, Levi, Vinokur etc. Compere Merle promises everyone a certificate for testing genius designer Yevgeny Nourish's new game *transCendenZ*, for manufacturer PilgrImage. Nourish tells Merle he's worried about the anti-game theme which must have come from the players. Allegra and Pikul remove guns from their dog's false coat, and kill Nourish and Merle. The Chinese guy raises his hands and says "...are we still in the game?"

Comment: eXistenZ is a waking dream, a surrealistic interface between human biology and technology, and another Cronenbergian investigation of levels of being: "All reality is virtual."

Themes: Cause And Effect: The game-within-a-game-within-'reality' is a chain of causative events, but is not easily (or definitively) deciphered. Frankenstein Syndrome/The Absent (Or Mad) Scientist: Testing Nourish's new game opens up a whole new Videodrome. The human nervous system is once more shown to be highly unpredictable. Mind/Body Schism: In the game scenario, the mind redefines the body; Allegra and Pikul both change their appearance and level of confidence. Despite being in a mental game-world, the danger to the body is very real. Altered States/Transformation: Is the game real? Is reality a game? Does transformation occur in one or the other, or both? Sharing a group 'reality' echoes *Scanners*. Postmodern/Existential Uncertainty: Narrative as pure uncertainty. What level of reality are we in at any one time? Are we in the game? Or another game altogether? Is the game world secure, or are unforeseen elements bleeding through from elsewhere? Do we begin and/or end in 'reality?' Viewers should be given their own Accumicon helmets. Body/Sexual Horror: The idea of linking subjective experiences via 'umbycords' plugged into the spine is designed to provoke minor revulsion. Bioports are sexually potent images. Illegal operations to fit spinal ports are akin to old-style backstreet abortions. Sexual ambiguity is ever-present; the scene where Gas fits Pikul's bioport carries heavy homo-erotic overtones. Allegra is a seductress who offers Pikul existential and sexual liberation from his repression. Slaying Sacred Cows: Society is again fractured and antagonistic; split into shallow, often incomprehensible dogmatic factions. Inspired by the fatwa against Salman Rushdie, the text is a treatise against fundamentalism of any kind. Secrets: As with many Cronenberg scenarios, so much is veiled, hidden, ambiguous or unknowable that one's subjective interpretation is all-important. Clues are laid, but certain pieces of the jigsaw are forever missing. Bizarre Organisations: Antenna Research, PilgrImage, Cortical Systematics, Realist Underground. Disease/Ageing/Death: Disease can arise through infected bioports (a metaphor for shared needles?) or can directly infect the organic game pods themselves - a whole new world of disease opens up through genetically-engineered virtual reality games. The trend of body alteration is taken to its logical extreme; merged with computer technology. And for what? To extend the boundaries of human knowledge? No, to play next-generation VR games. Cronenberg's scathing satire is always evident. Faithless: Cronenberg's philosophy comes through loud and clear, especially in dialogue relating to the rules of the 'game' (extracts quoted above). The relationship of the creator to the created is also questioned. Is the creator in control, or can the creation (game) develop levels of its own, beyond the creator's will? transCendenZ implies a fundamental(ist) religious trumping of mere eXistenZ.

Style: There is minimalism, which Cronenberg has used to great effect, and then there is the almost absent production design of *eXistenZ*. Designers' efforts to produce games of greater complexity with more spectacular graphics is totally reversed. This game world, while in one sense looking very real, in another is Philip K Dick's 'cardboard' world. Bare wooden buildings, labelled 'Motel' or 'Country Gas Station' exist alongside curiosities like the two-headed amphibian, which puzzles even the designer. Old fashioned rear-projection is used for backgrounds when driving. Although Cronenberg uses digital effects for the first time, the scene transitions are accomplished by subtle effects of mise en scène. 'Reality' is subtraction: no televisions, no phones, no computers, no jewellery, no watches, no suits, no ties, no stripes, no dots, just plain colours. The game world's incompleteness is minutely realised.

Trivia: After navigating the speculative universe of Philip K Dick in earlier films, Cronenberg makes his first outright homage; in the Motel room, Allegra and Pikul eat 'Perky Pat' fast food. This refers to elements in the novel *The Three Stigmata Of Palmer Eldritch*, a metaphysical examination of alternate realities and who controls them. The recurring conceit of the dog bringing or running off with bone guns is a rather unsubtle acknowledgement that this is ultimately a shaggy dog story. The twelve chairs and players of the game in the church hall has been interpreted as a reference to the Last Supper, but Cronenberg maintains it was accidental. Allegra's game pod container looks like a ski boot because it is one. After trying to come up with a similar design, Cronenberg decided to use the real thing. *eXistenZ* is a road map of existentialist philosophy (far too complex to discuss here; if you're keen, read introductions to Heidegger, Kierkegaard, Nietzsche and Sartre. Recommended fiction includes Sartre's *Nausea*, Camus' *The Outsider*, Kafka's *The Trial* and *The Castle*, Knut Hamsun's *Mysteries*, Hermann Hesse's *Steppenwolf*, Henri Barbusse's *Hell* and any Philip K Dick. Dick's *Ubik* probably approximates most closely to *eXistenZ*).

Verdict: I didn't much care for *eXistenZ* first time, but it has grown on me. Sure, all the usual Cronenberg ingredients and attributes are present, but they seemed somehow stale and lightweight. It is a playful film, which is part of the problem – I'd have liked it done Hollywood style; big budget, amazing effects, mega-action and dripping tension (*The Matrix* soon unexpectedly delivered the kind of film I had wanted). Best taken as a light introduction to Cronenberg's Universe, and a fun, clever science fiction movie, it's still a shame it doesn't add up to more. 3/5

10. Dead Zones: Forgotten Television Work

Filler material directed, scripted and photographed in France on 16mm by David Cronenberg for Canadian Broadcasting Corporation, 1971: *Jim Ritchie, Sculptor* – A Montreal sculptor living in France; *Letter From Michelangelo* – text by Michelangelo, voice-over by Paul Mulholland; *Tourettes* – A small village in southern France.

Filler material shot in Canada, 1972: *Don Valley; Fort York; In The Dirt; Lakeshore; Scarborough Bluffs; Winter Garden.* Approximately 5-minute fillers with music tracks only.

Secret Weapons (1971)

Director David Cronenberg; Screenplay Norman Snider
Cast: Barbara O'Kelly (Motorcycle Gang Leader), Norman Snider (The Scientist), Vernon Chapman (The Bureaucrat), Ronald Mlodzik, Bruce Martin, Tom Skudra, Moses Smith, Lister Sinclair (Commentary)
Credits: Production Company Emergent Films For The Canadian Broadcasting Corporation; Executive Producer Paddy Sampson; Associate Producer George Jonas; Cinematographer David Cronenberg; 27 minutes, 16mm colour, for *Program X,* transmitted 1st June 1972

"You are looking at a film shot in 1977 during the Civil War..." Giant drug conglomerate General Pharmaceuticals runs society, supplying aggression stimulants for troops to propagate the war. One of its meta-adrenaline research scientists, recalled for security vetting, pledges loyalty to company policy but refuses to hand over his research material. Ordered to attend a retreat run by the Holy Police, he escapes via a bout of psychic judo ("Much of what is happening on your screen is at a subverbal level") and encounters the resistance. To his surprise, it is a motorcycle gang led by a woman with a nihilistic desire for rebellion for its own sake. He is confronted by the disturbing consequences of his research.

Cronenberg has described *Secret Weapons* as his "suppressed" film. Its themes connect directly with *From The Drain*, *Stereo*, *Crimes Of The Future* and *Scanners*.

The Victim (1975)

Director David Cronenberg; Screenplay Ty Haller
Cast: Janet Wright (Lucy), Jonathan Welsh (Donald), Cedric Smith
Credits: Production Company Canadian Broadcasting Corporation; Executive Producer George Bloomfield; Producer Deborah Peaker; VT Photographer Eamon Beglan; VT Editor Garry Fisher; Art Director Nikolai Soloviov; Sound Brian Radford, Bill Dunn; Special Effects George Clarke; Sound Effects Olive St Sauveur; 27 minutes, 2" VT colour, for *Peepshow*, transmitted 22nd January 1976

Peepshow covered daring ground for its era: "Everywhere you go someone is watching you; you can't escape; there is nowhere to go; you can't escape; it's all a peepshow." Donald dials overweight loner Lucy's number at random from the directory, and attempts to impress her. Cronenberg voyeuristically examines the characters' quirks and environments; sinister Donald has posters for *Magnum Force* and *The Mechanic* on his wall, and wears a T-shirt for the yet-to-be-seen *Shivers*! News clippings of local rapes adorn a noticeboard, and the contents of his black leather bag remain a secret. Fetishization also extends to behaviour. Lucy crawls along and growls into the camera lens, crams cream cakes into her mouth, caresses a cat with her toes and runs her fingers along the 'shaft' of the receiver. Donald regards himself in a mirror as he fondles a pair of lace panties; while calling Lucy he has one hand beneath his bedsheet and opens a bottle of beer which spurts between his thighs. (The BBC wouldn't run this today!) His calls develop into threats, and he eventually breaks into her apartment. To his horror, he finds himself inside a gigantic cage; Lucy is a whip-wielding dominatrix who has turned the tables on him. Within the confines of episodic TV, Cronenberg manages to transgress the limits of the medium and introduce *Videodrome*'s S & M fetishism.

The Lie Chair (1975)

Director David Cronenberg; Screenplay David Cole
Cast: Richard Monette (Neil), Susan Hogan (Carol), Amelia Hall (Mildred), Doris Petrie (Mrs Rogers)
Credits: Production Company Canadian Broadcasting Corporation; Executive Producer George Bloomfield; Producer Eoin Sprott; VT Photographer Eamon Beglan; Sound Roland Huebsche, Bill Dunn; Set Designer Rudi Dorn; 27 minutes, 2" VT colour, for *Peepshow*, transmitted 12th February 1976

The old, stale story about a couple whose car breaks down on a stormy night. Seeking help at an isolated house shared by two old ladies, they stay the night and soon discover the women are not quite what they seem. After taking over the identities of the women's dead grandchildren, they finally enter an idyllic fiction of family life. With no cliché left unturned, this is strictly for the paycheque.

The Italian Machine (1976)

Director/Screenplay David Cronenberg
Cast: Gary McKeehan (Lionel), Frank Moore (Fred), Hardee Linehan (Bug), Chuck Shamata (Reinhardt), Louis Negin (Mouette), Toby Tarnow (Lana), Geza Kovacs (Riccardo), Cedric Smith (Luke)
Credits: Production Company Canadian Broadcasting Corporation; Executive Producer Stephen Patrick; Cinematographer Nicholas Evdemon; Editor David Denovan; Sound Tom Bilenky; Art Director Peter Douet; 28 minutes, 16mm colour, for *Teleplay*, transmitted December 1976

Lionel, Fred and Bug are motorcycle fanatics who relax listening to audio recordings of Isle Of Man TT races. They are furious to learn that hated local bike dealer Reinhardt has sold a legendary Ducati Desmo Super Sport to art collector Edgar Mouette. Posing as journalists for *Techno Art World* magazine, they discover the bike is displayed as a 'sculpture' in Mouette's house. Lionel asks "How could he look at it and not want to make it *go*?" Mouette and his wife Lana also keep a 'non-person,' Riccardo, as a live art object. Lionel bribes Riccardo with cocaine to offer Mouette a conceptual 'deal' – one piece of art purchases another for a symbolic fee. Persuaded of its novelty appeal to New York modern art magazines, Mouette accepts and Riccardo hands over a dollar for the Ducati. Lana acquires a new non-person and everyone lives happily ever after.

Cronenberg's passion for motor sport was later showcased in *Fast Company*, but *The Italian Machine* is much more interesting, satirising shallow social values and provocatively stirring the art vs commerce debate. Fetishising the beautiful bike comes a poor second to fulfilling its function, as an exquisitely engineered performance machine. Four cast members reappeared in Cronenberg movies; Smith in *Fast Com-*

pany, McKeehan in *The Brood*, Moore in *Rabid* and Kovacs in *Scanners* and *The Dead Zone*.

Friday The 13th Episode 12: Faith Healer (1987)

Director David Cronenberg; Teleplay Christine Cornish
Credits: Production Company Paramount Television Inc; Executive Producer Frank Mancuso Jr; Producer Iain Paterson; 26 minutes, colour

An unremarkable entry in the Cronenberg canon. Old hand Bob Silverman plays a character suffering from a terminal disease. After *The Brood* and *Scanners*, he was used to it.

In 1989 and 1990, Cronenberg directed a number of 30-second commercials for The Partners' Film Company Ltd: Ontario Hydro – *Hot Showers, Laundry, Cleaners, Timers*; Cadbury Caramilk – *Bistro, Surveillance*; Nike International – *Transformations*.

Scales Of Justice: Regina Vs Horvath (1990)

Director David Cronenberg; Screenplay Michael Tait, George Jonas
Credits: Production Company Canadian Broadcasting Corporation, In Association With Scales Of Justice Enterprises Inc; Executive Producer Carol Reynolds; Producer George Jonas; Photographer Rodney Charters; Supervising Editor Ronald Sanders; Music Howard Shore; Sound Bryan Day; Production Designer Carol Spier; 48 minutes, Betacam colour

Scales Of Justice: Regina Vs Logan (1990)

Director David Cronenberg; Screenplay Gabriel Emmanuel, George Jonas
Credits: Production Company Canadian Broadcasting Corporation, In Association With Scales Of Justice Enterprises Inc; Executive Producer Carol Reynolds; Producer George Jonas; Photographer Rodney Charters; Supervising Editor Ronald Sanders; Music Howard Shore; Sound Bryan Day; Production Designer Carol Spier; 44 minutes, Betacam colour

The *Scales Of Justice* series dramatises actual court cases. The Horvath case dates from 1970s British Columbia, when a woman's 17-year-old son confesses to her murder. Questions arise about the methods used by detective Proke to extract the confession – interrogation or hypnosis? Cronenberg regular Les Carlson plays the clever cop. The Logan case took place in Toronto, in 1980. During a store hold-up, a cashier is shot and paralysed. The cashier, Barbara Turnbull, stars as herself.

11. References & Notes

Books

Crash by Iain Sinclair, UK: British Film Institute Modern Classics, 1999, 128 pages, £7.99, ISBN 085170719

Crash screenplay by David Cronenberg, UK: Faber And Faber, 1996, 65 pages, £7.99, ISBN 0571191274

Cronenberg On Cronenberg edited by Chris Rodley, UK: Faber And Faber, 1997 (revised edition) 230 pages, £9.99, ISBN 0571191371

David Cronenberg: A Delicate Balance by Peter Morris, Canada: ECW Press, 1994, ISBN 1550221914

David Cronenberg edited by Wayne Drew, UK: British Film Institute (Dossier 21), 1984, 57 pages

David Cronenberg's eXistenZ: A Graphic Novel by David Cronenberg & Sean Scoffield (Illus), UK: Key Porter Books, 1999, 128 pages, £13.99, ISBN 1552630277

Everything Is Permitted – The Making Of Naked Lunch edited by Ira Silverberg, UK: Grafton, 1992, 128 pages, £9.99, ISBN 0586217142

The Shape Of Rage – The Films Of David Cronenberg edited by Piers Handling, Canada: Academy Of Canadian Cinema/General Publishing Co, 1983, 217 pages, ISBN 0773611371

Selected Articles

Cinefantastique:

Lee Rolfe, 'David Cronenberg On *Rabid*', Vol 6 No 3, 1977, p. 26

Paul M Sammon, 'David Cronenberg', Vol 10 No 4, 1981, pp. 21-34

Tim Lucas, '*Videodrome*', Vol 12 No 2/3, 1981, pp. 4-7

Tim Lucas, '*Videodrome*', Vol 14 No 2, 1983/4, pp. 32-49

Tim Lucas, '*The Dead Zone*', Vol 14 No 2, 1983/4, pp. 24-31, 60-61

Bruce Kirkland, '*The Fly*', Vol 16 No 3, 1986, pp. 15, 60

Gary Kimber, 'David Cronenberg's *The Naked Lunch*', Vol 22 No 4, 1992, pp. 12-13

Gary Kimber, 'Filming *Naked Lunch*', Vol 22 No 5, 1992, pp. 8-19

Paul Wardle, 'David Cronenberg Goes "*Crash*"', Vol 28 No10, 1997, pp. 26-31

Patricia Moir, '*Crash* Review', Vol 28 No 11, 1997, pp. 59-61

Cinefex:

Tim Lucas, '*The Fly* Papers', No 28, 1986, pp. 4-29
Don Shay, 'Double Vision' [on *Dead Ringers*], No 36, 1988, pp. 32-49
Jody Duncan, 'Borrowed Flesh' [on *Naked Lunch*], No 49, 1992, pp. 24-39

Fantastic Films:

Carol Sherman, 'Reality vs. Reali-TV' [on *Videodrome*], No 33, 1983, pp. 48-50

Videos

Many of Cronenberg's movies are deleted, but do try the plethora of auction sites and Z-shops on the net.

David Cronenberg Collection (*Shivers*/*Rabid*/*The Brood* triple pack), 0585543, £13.99
The Brood, 0576743, £5.99
Crash, CVR75095, £15.99
Dead Ringers, 3037060343, £5.99
The Dead Zone, 0858823, deleted
eXistenZ, AA019S, £14.99
Firestarter/*The Dead Zone*, CVI1543, deleted (only uncut UK version)
The Fly, 1503BD, £5.99
Friday's Curse – The Electrocutioner/*Faith Healer*, VHB2291, deleted
M. Butterfly, V012984, deleted
Naked Lunch, VA30567, deleted
Naked Lunch (widescreen), VA30298, deleted
Rabid, 0576723, £5.99
Scanners, 0576683, £5.99
Shivers, 0576703, £5.99
Videodrome, 0782983, £5.99

DVDs

The Brood, FCD063, £15.99
Crash, CDR25095, £19.99
Dead Ringers, 3711500293, £9.99
eXistenZ, AA019DVD, £19.99
Scanners, FCD064, £15.99

Useful Websites:

Quite a few, here are the best:

The New Flesh Directory (DC Homepage) –
  http://zappa.users.netlink.co.uk/cronen.html
Cronendrome –
  http://members.dencity.com/cronendrome/Index2.html
Essay *Psychoplasmics: Body Mutation And Dualism In The Films Of David Cronenberg* –
  http://www.uncarved.demon.co.uk/2012/psycho.html
  http://user.chollian.net/~cynicult/cronen.html
  http://freespace.virgin.net/kevinbishop3/index.html

Most have links to these sites and others. Also take a look at individual film sites like http://www.existenz.com, and of course the ever-useful Internet Movie Database at http://www.imdb.com

1983 Science Fiction Retrospective

Cronenberg's selection for the Toronto Film Festival was predictably provocative, extending the boundaries of most people's definition of science fiction:

L'Age D'or – director Luis Buñuel
Alphaville – Jean-Luc Godard
The Bed Sitting Room – Richard Lester
The Cabinet Of Dr Caligari – Robert Wiene
Creature From The Black Lagoon – Jack Arnold
The Devils – Ken Russell
Don't Look Now – Nicolas Roeg
Dr Strangelove – Stanley Kubrick
Duel – Steven Spielberg
The Fearless Vampire Killers – Roman Polanski
Forbidden Planet – Fred MacLeod Wilcox
Freaks – Tod Browning
Le Golem – Julien Duvivier
Helen Of Troy – Robert Wise
I Killed Einstein, Gentlemen! – Oldrich Lipsky
The Incredible Shrinking Man – Jack Arnold
Je t'aime, je t'aime – Alain Resnais
La Jetée – Chris Marker

Lord Of The Flies – Peter Brook
M – Fritz Lang
Mad Love – Karl Freund
On The Beach – Stanley Kramer
Peeping Tom – Michael Powell
Performance – Nicolas Roeg/Donald Cammell
Private Parts – Paul Bartel
Satyricon – Federico Fellini
Taxi Driver – Martin Scorsese
Things To Come – William Cameron Menzies
This Island Earth – Joseph Newman
Toby Dammit – Federico Fellini
Un Chien Andalou – Luis Buñuel
The Unholy Three – Tod Browning
Vampyr – Carl Dreyer
Vargtimmen [The Hour Of The Wolf] – Ingmar Bergman
War Of The Worlds – Byron Haskin
Zéro de Conduite – Jean Vigo

Cronenberg's introductory notes make interesting reading:

Taxi Driver – a better *Blade Runner* than *Blade Runner*. New York is a
  nightmare LA/Tokyo of the future. De Niro is a sleepless alien who
  does a poor job of passing himself off as an earthling. He can't really
  figure out human sexuality but he wants to get involved anyway. It
  doesn't work.
Peeping Tom – a mad scientist creates a monster who kills. The scientist
  is the director of the movie and the monster is a camera.
L'Age D'or/Un Chien Andalou – surrealists Luis Buñuel and Salvador
  Dali were much influenced by Freud, but was Freud a scientist or a
  poet?
Helen Of Troy – *The Iliad* has always been an important model for the
  sci-fi sub-genre known as 'space opera.' *Helen Of Troy* could be
  plugged right into the *Star Wars* saga. It features exotic castles, strange
  machines, prophecy, magical powers, bizarre warriors. Is the Force
  with Helen?

Stillbirths

An exhaustive list of the movies that Cronenberg has been offered and/or turned down would be impossible, but here are some tasty ones...

The Big One. Hope he does it sometime; some might say he's been doing it for years. "Pierre David came up to me one day and said, 'Listen to this. Just listen. And tell me what you think... *David Cronenberg's Frankenstein.*' So I said, 'Sounds good to me. What about poor Mary Shelley?'"

Beverly Hills Cop (With Sylvester Stallone)

Top Gun (Or, *Top Guns* as it was then)

Witness (Or, *Called Home*. Cronenberg couldn't empathise with the Amish, whom he saw as repressive)

Flashdance (I kid you not)

Total Recall (After Fred Schepisi, Richard Rush and Bruce Beresford, and before Paul Verhoeven)

And, most amazing of all, *Return Of The Jedi*! I can see it now: Jabba the Talking Asshole; Luke and Leia as Siamese twins; the Ewoks as psychosexual vampires and Darth Vader as a hard-core S&M fetishist. I'd buy that for a dollar!

The Essential Library

Enjoyed this book? Then try some other titles in the Essential library.

New This Month: **David Cronenberg** by John Costello
                     Slasher Movies by Mark Whitehead

Also Available:

Film: **Woody Allen** by Martin Fitzgerald
          Jane Campion by Ellen Cheshire
          Jackie Chan by Michelle Le Blanc & Colin Odell
          The Brothers Coen by John Ashbrook & Ellen Cheshire
          Film Noir by Paul Duncan
          Terry Gilliam by John Ashbrook
          Heroic Bloodshed edited by Martin Fitzgerald
          Alfred Hitchcock by Paul Duncan
          Krzysztof Kieslowski by Monika Maurer
          Stanley Kubrick by Paul Duncan
          David Lynch by Michelle Le Blanc & Colin Odell
          Steve McQueen by Richard Luck
          Brian De Palma by John Ashbrook
          Sam Peckinpah by Richard Luck
          Vampire Films by Michelle Le Blanc & Colin Odell
          Orson Welles by Martin Fitzgerald

TV: **Doctor Who** by Mark Campbell
          The Simpsons by Peter Mann

Books: **Noir Fiction** by Paul Duncan

Available at all good bookstores at £2.99 each, or send a cheque to: **Pocket Essentials (Dept DC), 18 Coleswood Rd, Harpenden, Herts, AL5 1EQ, UK** Please make cheques payable to 'Oldcastle Books.' Add 50p postage & packing for each book in the UK and £1 elsewhere.

US customers can send $5.95 plus $1.95 postage & packing for each book to **Trafalgar Square Publishing, PO Box 257, Howe Hill Road, North Pomfret, Vermont 05053, USA**. tel: 802-457-1911, fax: 802-457-1913, e-mail: tsquare@sover.net

Customers worldwide can order online at **www.pocketessentials.com**, **www.amazon.com** and at all good online bookstores.